THE
SIZZLING SOUTHWESTERN
COOKBOOK

THE SIZZLING SOUTHWESTERN COOKBOOK

Hot and Zesty, Light and Healthy
Chile Cuisine

by

LYNN NUSOM

LOWELL HOUSE - LOS ANGELES
CONTEMPORARY BOOKS - CHICAGO

Library of Congress Cataloging-in-Publication Data

Nusom, Lynn.
    The sizzling southwestern cookbook / Lynn Nusom.
        p. cm.
    Includes index.
    ISBN 1-56565-210-X
    1. Cookery (Peppers) 2. Cookery, American—Southwestern style. I. Title.
TX803.P46N87
641.6'384—dc20   94-35379
                                             CIP

Lowell House books can be purchased at special discounts when ordered in bulk for premiums and special sales. Contact Department VH at the address below.

Requests for such permissions should be addressed to:
Lowell House
2029 Century Park East, Suite 3290
Los Angeles, CA 90067

Publisher: Jack Artenstein
General Manager, Lowell House Adult: Bud Sperry
Text Design: Nancy Freeborn

Manufactured in the United States of America
10 9 8 7 6 5 4 3 2 1

This book is dedicated to my wife, Guylyn Morris Nusom, an accomplished recipe designer, food stylist, and author in her own right.

Without her help in choosing, testing, tasting, and critiquing the recipes, this book would never have come to be.

THE AUTHOR

LYNN NUSOM, former advertising and marketing executive, businessman, chef, and restaurateur, is passionate about life and especially about food and cooking.

"I try to be innovative in my cooking, keeping in mind that the dish should be a feast for the eyes as well as the taste buds," says the author of nine books on the history, cooking, and travel opportunities of the Southwest.

The author and his wife, Guylyn Morris Nusom, live in Las Cruces, New Mexico, with four dogs and a cat all named after foods or chefs.

In addition to his duties as the food editor of the local paper, writing cookbooks and articles on food and travel, starring in cooking videos, and making television appearances, the Nusoms also own and operate Lynn Nusom's Kitchen, a catering service.

TABLE OF CONTENTS

THE SIZZLING SOUTHWESTERN COOKBOOK

This book contains low-fat variations of classic southwestern recipes and daring, new, and different dishes using chile in both subtle and dramatic ways.

A
CHILE
PRIMER

INTRODUCTION

I love food and cooking and have spent my life trying to learn the best methods of preparing the tastiest, most pleasing dishes for myself, my family, and friends. My first cooking instructors were my paternal grandfather, who owned a hotel and was his own chef, and my maternal grandmother, who was a superb cook and who never measured anything in her large farmhouse kitchen.

As a teenager I was introduced to Mexican and southwestern cooking when I visited one of my aunts and my grandmother, who were longtime Arizona residents. For a while I excelled at making drugstore chili. When I worked in the motion picture industry, I even toted the ingredients to Manhattan and Europe to recreate it whenever anyone asked.

While I was working in the movie business, my superiors discovered my interest and talent in food and I was soon planning and overseeing parties and movie premieres. It was at this time I learned that giving parties was my forte.

But it wasn't until I married my wife, Guylyn Morris Nusom, and we settled first in Tucson, Arizona, and then in New Mexico that I began to experience the true delights of southwestern cooking—in particular, recipes featuring chile.

Like many converts I not only appreciated all the chile dishes I found offered but began to admire the charm and appeal that chile could offer to all sorts of other recipes. I also decided, with all the arrogance of an outsider, that the southwestern dishes made with chile were limited —at least the ones I had sampled.

Since I had studied food and cooking in New York, taking courses in classic French and northern Italian cuisine, and honed these skills in Europe, it seemed natural to try to marry the European methods and ingredients with what the Southwest had to offer.

At one point friends and relatives knew that no matter what was on the menu, from vichyssoise to crème brûlée, somehow I'd find a way to put green chile in it. My wife, a lifelong southwesterner and an avid fan of red chile, gradually, and sometimes gently, took me in hand and showed me the delights of red chile as well.

I've included low-fat versions and adaptations of classic southwestern recipes such as ceviche and chile rellenos. And I've also created other new recipes that fit the southwestern lifestyle and palate.

The tolerance to chile varies from individual to individual. If you are a novice when it comes to cooking and eating chile, you may want to reduce the quantities of chile I call for in the recipes. As you gain more confidence in eating the fiery peppers, or if you are already a "chile head" or a connoisseur of red and green chile and you find that a dish is not hot enough for your liking, feel free to add a little more.

Of course, when combined with other ingredients chiles produce different heat levels depending on the type and amount of other food in the recipe. For instance, a salsa made with three or four vegetables or fruits and a couple of finely chopped jalapeños will be a great deal hotter than the same number of jalapeños added to three or four quarts of soup.

A CHILE PRIMER

It is no secret: Fat makes food taste good! We know now, however, that although it tastes good, a lot of fat is not good for us. So in order to improve the taste of food, we look to other ingredients as substitutes for fat. In this quest I've found that one of the greatest flavor enhancers and replacements for fat in many recipes is chile.

Although chile has long been the favorite spice of cooks in the Southwest, it has only been the past few years that "chile-mania" has swept the country.

The history of chile is as fascinating and as colorful as the different kinds of chiles themselves. Chile, a wild perennial, is native to the tropical regions of the Americas and was originally grown in South America and Mexico. Although most historians agree that Columbus brought the first chile back to Europe in 1493, there is some debate as to how chile wound up in the Southwest. Did the Pueblo Indians of North America trade chile seeds with the Toltecs of central Mexico? Or did the Spaniards bring the first chile seeds to the Southwest in the late 16th century?

The controversy about chile does not end there. The very spelling of *chile* is often in dispute. I recently submitted a long travel article to a publisher in which I talked about the food and eating habits of the people in southern New Mexico. When the editor sent the copy back, the word *chile* had been painstakingly changed to *chili*.

After many conversations with the editor, I sent copies of newspaper articles and excerpts from books written by southwesterners and about the Southwest in which the word was spelled *chile* with an *e* when referring to the vegetable itself, and *chili* with an *i* when referring to a dish—usually consisting of stewed meat, with tomatoes and sometimes beans. I concluded my argument by saying that if the finished article was published with *chile* spelled *chili*, I would be forced to move out of New Mexico. The editor was extremely gracious and, not wanting to cause me the expense and pain of finding another area of the country to live in, bowed to my wishes and spelled it *chile*—the only way that New Mexicans are comfortable with.

The spelling of *chile* has even prompted a "war" between Texas and New Mexico, with Texas opting for *chili*. This war is fought every year at festivals where chile producers and manufacturers of chile products display their wares and chili cooks create stews made with chile.

Whether you spell it with an *e* or an *i,* many chile lovers claim that with its wide range of flavor and heat, chile is addictive.

It is an odorless, invisible substance in the flesh of the chile pod, capsaicin, that makes the chile hot and inflicts a fiery, sometimes seemingly unbearable pain in the mouth. This is followed by a wave of relief caused by endorphins, the natural painkillers the body releases to quell the fire. Many people call this alternating pain and relief "mouth-surfing."

Whether you want to cut down on fat in your diet and add some excitement to those low-fat recipes, simply enjoy the taste of hot food, like to experience new and different tastes, or want to go mouth-surfing, try the myriad kinds of chile that will make your cooking and eating an exciting adventure.

SELECTING AND PROCESSING CHILE

In general chiles are green while growing. As they ripen they usually turn into a wide range of colors depending on the variety, including yellow, orange, red, and brown.

Some chiles, such as the New Mexico green, Anaheim, and jalapeño, are still green when fully ripe. When these chiles turn red they are in an advanced stage of ripeness. In recipes these chiles are often referred to as New Mexico green, New Mexico red, Anaheim green, Anaheim red, and so on, to denote the stage of ripeness to be used.

When you buy fresh chile, look for fruits that are firm, dry, and heavy for their size. The skin of the chile should be unblemished, smooth, and shiny. If the chile is wrinkled it is old.

Fresh chile does not keep for long periods of time, although they will usually hold for up to a week in the vegetable bin of your refrigerator. If left at room temperature they will rapidly shrivel and spoil.

When handling fresh chile it is advisable to wear rubber gloves and immediately wash any areas of your body that come into contact with the chile. Never rub your eyes when handling chile.

Some fresh chiles may be eaten raw, without roasting or cooking. Jalapeños are delectable this way, especially if the flesh is finely chopped. Although most people roast poblanos, Anaheims, and New Mexico chiles before eating them, I have found that a very fresh poblano, if finely diced (usually in a food processor fitted with a steel blade), is delicious in some recipes. It is not, as is generally thought, tough. I have even used New Mexico green and Anaheim chiles in the raw state—only for special recipes and with the flesh minutely diced. The dicing is well worth the trouble, as the taste can be delicious. If you use chiles raw, they must be eaten immediately; they do not keep.

Longtime residents of the Southwest will often buy green chiles daily, take them home, and use a rack or a long-tined fork to roast them over an open gas flame to have the chile ready for that day's lunch or dinner. Other methods for preparing small amounts of chile include roasting them over a charcoal or gas grill, and roasting them in the oven on an ungreased baking sheet. Purveyors throughout the Southwest roast chile for their customers and sell it in bulk.

In the area of New Mexico where we live, there is no more glorious aroma in late summer or early fall than the wonderful smell of chile roasting all over the countryside. If you buy chile that has been roasted by a store, it will usually be packed in a burlap bag. When you get home, immediately wet several clean towels with cold water, place them on an outdoor table, lay the still-hot peppers on them, and cover with more wet towels to let the chile steam. Then, using rubber gloves, peel the blackened skin off the chile. Use what you can right away and freeze the rest. Unless you add vinegar or citrus juice to the chile, it will not keep in the refrigerator for more than a day or two.

 # GUIDE TO CHILE

The following is a guide to the different types of chile used in this book, their attributes, and their rating on the heat scale, with 10 denoting the most fire.

Fresh Chiles

ANAHEIM CHILE: This type is closely related to the New Mexico varieties of chile, and although for years it was classified as a separate type, some experts now classify it under the heading, New Mexico chile. Although they originally acquired the name Anaheim because they were grown in the Anaheim area of southern California, they are now grown all over the Southwest.

The plants are very productive. The fruit grows to 6 or 7 inches in length and usually measure from 2 to 2½ inches in diameter.

This is a firm, thick-fleshed chile with a bright, fresh flavor that improves when the fruit is roasted.

Green Anaheims are at their best when used in salsas, sauces, and soups. They are also delightful when stuffed with rice, cheese, or meat.

The ripe, red form of the green Anaheim is sweeter. It is excellent in salsas and soups and is superb pickled.

Heat Scale: 2–3

BELL PEPPERS: Although most people do not think of bell peppers as chile because they are usually not hot, they are the most common variety of chile grown and used in the United States.

The sweet, thick-fleshed peppers are 3 to 5 inches long and 4 to 5 inches in diameter and probably got their name from their bell-like shape. Although in many parts of the country only green bell peppers were commonly available in the past, you can now buy yellow, orange, red, and purple varieties.

They are great eaten raw in salads or as crudités and can be used in innumerable cooked dishes including stir-frys, casseroles, or vegetable dishes. They are also superb as backdrops and hosts to their hotter cousins, such as the Anaheim and New Mexico chile. Teamed with jalapeños or serranos, they fill out a salsa and temper the heat, and they are great grilled as a complement to meat or seafood.

Heat Scale: 0

GÜERO, HUNGARIAN WAX, or **BANANA CHILE:** Güero is the Spanish generic term for yellow chiles. This medium-fleshed chile varies from 3 to 5 inches in length and from 1 to 1½ inches in diameter. It has a sharp, slightly sweet taste and is best as an accent in sauces or salad dressing or included in an escabeche.

Heat Scale: 4.5–6.5

HABANERO: One of the hottest of all chiles, this chile is primarily grown and used in Central America and the Caribbean. Although not used much in southwestern cooking, it is growing in popularity among "chile-heads."

The fruit measures approximately 2 inches long and 1¼ to 1¾ inches in diameter and is wide at the top and tapers to a rounded bottom.

Use the habanero with extra care—a little goes a long way!

Heat Scale: 10

JALAPEÑO: This green or red chile is the most popular hot chile consumed in the United States. The name derives from the city of Jalapa in Veracruz, Mexico. The color of jalapeños ranges from a deep, bright green to a dark green to gold, orange, and a deep red when fully ripe.

Jalapeños measure from 2 to 3 inches long and 1 to 1½ inches in diameter and have a thick flesh and a sharp, fresh green flavor that goes with practically anything—soups, bread, salsas, dips, pizza, pasta, and even desserts such as ice cream and apple pie.

In addition to fresh jalapeños you can also buy canned or pickled jalapeños either whole or in slices or rings.

Heat Scale: 5.5

MANZANA: A thin-fleshed yellow-orange pepper also called chile caballo, chile peron, and chile rocoto, it measures approximately 3 inches in length and 2 to 2¼ inches in diameter. This is a hot chile used in sauces and salsas or mixed vegetable dishes.

Heat Scale: 6–8

NEW MEXICO CHILE: A wide variety of chiles are grown under the New Mexico label:

Sandia, a hot variety about 4 on the heat scale.

New Mexico 6–4 (also called *NuMex 6–4*), one of the most popular New Mexican varieties and used a great deal by chile processors. It is 3 on the heat scale.

NuMex Big Jim, the largest of the New Mexican varieties, with pods that can grow up to 12 inches long. They are ideal for making chile rellenos and their heat scale rating is 2.

NuMex R. Naky, developed by the late Roy Nakayama at New Mexico State University, this is a mild chile of about 2 on the heat scale. It is very popular in southwestern New Mexico.

The New Mexican green chiles have an earthy, sweet flavor. Although similar to the Anaheim chile in looks (except for the NuMex R. Naky), they are usually hotter.

With their clean, sharp flavor New Mexico chiles can be used in a host of different ways: salsas, soups, pasta dishes, sliced on hamburgers or other sandwiches, stuffed, in dips, pizzas, tortas, frittatas, omelets, stews, casseroles, or as an accent to meat dishes.

New Mexico chile is great either green or red and freezes extremely well. You can also buy canned New Mexico green chile; although not as good as the fresh or frozen, it is perfectly acceptable in a pinch.

PIMENTO: Possessing more flavor than a bell pepper, the pimento is a heart-shaped chile that runs in color from bright red to scarlet and measures approximately 4 inches long and 2½ to 3 inches in diameter. I have bought pimentos that were as small as 2 inches long that were sweet and delicious.

Pimentos are great in salads and salsas, used as a garnish, or grilled with poultry or fish. They are also available canned in both water and oil and are used to stuff olives. Paprika is pimento ground into powder.

Heat Scale: 0–1

POBLANO: More popular in Mexico than the United States, this chile is gaining in prominence in the Southwest, especially in California. It is very dark green, sometimes with a purple-black tinge. A thick-fleshed variety, it varies in length from 4 to 5 inches and in diameter from 2½ to 3 inches.

Although most experts say that poblanos should always be roasted before eating, in some recipes in this book I use them raw. If chopped very finely they are fantastic in salsas or salad dressings. You must eat the dish right away, however, as the raw poblano will not keep.

The most favored uses of roasted poblanos are as chile rellenos and in moles, soups, and sauces.

Heat Scale: 3

SERRANO: This is a fiery chile 1 to 3 inches long, from ½ to ¾ inch in diameter, tapering to a point. It has a thick flesh with high acidity and has a definite bite to it. Used raw in escabeches and salsas, this chile is also good roasted and used in soups and sauces.

Heat Scale: 7

Dried Chiles

ANCHO: This is the dried poblano chile. Its color ranges from a dark brick red to cordovan. The ancho (which means "wide" in Spanish) is aptly named for its heart shape and broad top, which measures about 4 inches across.

The ancho is a sweet dried chile that evokes memories of raisins, coffee, and tobacco. Buy anchos when they are flexible and store the aromatic peppers until use. They keep well in glass jars in dry climates, but you may find that it is necessary to keep them refrigerated in more humid climates.

This dried chile is great in moles, sauces, and soups. Ancho is also available in some stores in powder form.

Heat Scale: 3–5

ÁRBOL (de Árbol): *Árbol* means "tree" in Spanish. These chiles are popularly called rooster beaks or rat's tails in Mexico as they are long and narrow and have a sharp hook or claw at the end.

The árbol has a scorching heat and is used in stews, soups, and meat or poultry dishes.
Heat Scale: 7.5–8

CASCABEL: This dark reddish brown chile is named after the Spanish word for rattle because the pods rattle when shaken. It has a smoky, nutty taste and is terrific used in soups, sauces, and salsas.

Heat Scale: 4

CAYENNE: This bright red pepper has a sharp bite to it. Crushed cayenne is sometimes used as flavoring for soups. Generally cayenne can only be bought in the powdered form. Use it in any dish where you want heat.

Heat Scale: 8

CHIPOTLE: These chiles are dried and smoked jalapeños. They are brown to black in color and run from 2 to 4 inches in length and approximately 1 inch across. They provide a deep, rich flavor to soups, salsas, and sauces such as adobo. Although you can buy them canned, they are not terribly good. I advise using the dried ones.

Heat Scale: 5–6

GUAJILLO: Orange-red in color with hints of brown, this long (4- to 6-inch) dried chile is sweet and hot and is used in salsas and soups.

Heat Scale: 2–4

MIRASOL: Some of the pods of this chile grow upright; the name is Spanish for "looking at the sun." This chile has a wonderful nutty flavor and is good in meat dishes, sauces, and stews.
　　Heat Scale: 5

NEW MEXICO RED: Crisp, clean heat defines this popular southwestern chile. The reds can be the ripe form of any of the green New Mexico varieties (see New Mexico chile under Fresh Chiles), and so the heat rating runs from mild to hot.
　　The chiles are sold whole by the pound or in packages and also as crushed flakes or ground into powder.
　　I use ground New Mexico red chile powder a great deal in my cooking. Do not confuse this with the "chili powder" sold in bottles and cans in supermarkets. The commercial product usually contains cumin, oregano, salt, garlic, and additives such as tricalcium phosphate. In contrast, New Mexico red chile powder is pure chile. It is sold in supermarkets and convenience stores throughout the Southwest and can be found in gourmet stores and specialty food shops in the rest of the country.
　　Heat Scale: 2–5, depending on the type of chile it is made of

PASADO: The pasado is a New Mexico or Anaheim red chile, roasted, peeled, and then dried. Traditionally the chile was preserved in this manner by Mexicans and Indians for use in the winter season. The heat from this chile loiters on the tongue.
　　Heat Scale: 5

PASILLA: The name means "little raisin" in Spanish. Also known as chile negro, this is a dark brown, wrinkled chile. It is one of the chiles used in mole and is also excellent in seafood dishes and sauces.
　　Heat Scale: 3–5

PEQUÍN (chile pequín): This wonderful chile has a searing heat that does not last. It is extremely popular throughout the Southwest, especially among chile aficionados.
　　The name most likely comes from the small size of the fruit. All sorts of legends and folklore surround this chile, including a belief by some Indians that it is a protection against evil spirits.
　　I love using this chile in all sorts of dishes: pasta, corn dishes, salsa, sauces, salad dressings, soups, with chicken, and to flavor vinegars and oils.
　　Heat Scale: 8–8.5

PULLA: This is a deep red, long chile that tapers to a point. It has a dusty, dry heat with overtones of licorice and cherry. Great for soups and salsas.
　　Heat Scale: 6

TEPÍN: This smaller, round, pea-shaped form of the pequín chile floods the mouth with intense heat that leaves quickly. This chile has a dusty flavor that works well with soups and salsas.
Heat Scale: 8–9

OTHER SOUTHWESTERN INGREDIENTS

For the most part I have used ingredients in these recipes that most southwestern cooks are familiar with and stock in their kitchens. For readers who may be new to this style of cooking, the following is a guide to typical southwestern ingredients.

BLUE CORN (blue corn tortillas, blue corn chips): Blue corn has been grown by the Pueblo Indians in the Southwest for centuries, but only recently has it become extremely popular with a wide range of southwestern cooks. You can use blue cornmeal to make tortillas, pancakes, or cornbread. You can also buy packaged blue cornmeal chips in supermarkets and specialty food stores.

CILANTRO: A broad-leaf member of the parsley family (and sometimes called Chinese parsley), cilantro is considered by most cooks to be essential to southwestern cooking. It is found in most grocery stores. Be sure to buy cilantro that is nice and green and has no yellow on the leaves. Cilantro keeps for a week if you place the stems in a clean jar with approximately an inch of water and store in the refrigerator.

Cilantro has a strong, earthy flavor and is at its best with tomatoes, chile, and fish and meat of all types.

CORIANDER: The coriander seed is from the same plant as the cilantro leaf. Also an integral part of southwestern cuisine, it is most often used ground in chilis, stews, soups, and salsas. You can find ground coriander in many supermarkets or specialty food stores.

CUMIN: Another must ingredient in southwestern food, ground cumin has a nutty flavor that complements chilis, salsas, and beans. You can buy ground cumin (labeled *comino* in Mexican markets) in supermarkets. You can also buy the raw seed in specialty stores and grind it yourself.

GROUND OREGANO: Although fresh and dried oregano leaves are common in many types of cooking, ground oregano is one of the most popular spices used in southwestern cooking. It is a must in many soups, stews, and chilis.

HOMINY: Hominy is kernels of corn that have been soaked in slaked lime in order to remove the hulls. Manufacturers use both white and yellow corn; I prefer to use the white when possible.

Hominy is an essential ingredient of posole, a traditional southwestern soup-stew. It is also wonderful mixed with other vegetables and in soups and chili.

JÍCAMA: A brown-skinned root vegetable used throughout Mexico and the Southwest. It is best peeled and julienned for a crudité tray, sliced and used in salads, or sprinkled with lime juice and red chile powder as an appetizer. Smaller jícamas tend to be sweeter than the larger ones.

MEXICAN CHOCOLATE: The brand of this grainy chocolate I use is Ibarra. It comes in an octagonal red and yellow box and contains sugar, cacao nibs, almonds, cinnamon, and lecithin. You can find this wonderful addition to moles and chilis in Mexican food markets or in specialty food stores.

NOPALES: The pads of the prickly pear cactus, nopales have a very fresh, green taste somewhere between a bell pepper and a tart green bean. Scrub off the prickles with a brush before using.

Nopales are great in salads, stir-frys, and in vegetable dishes. Although you can buy them canned, I have not found that they work well. Fresh is best.

PIÑONS: Grown throughout the Southwest on the high desert mesas, piñon nuts are prized for their delicate, nutty flavor. Difficult to gather and shell, they are expensive but well worth it. If you cannot find New Mexico or Arizona piñons you can substitute Italian or Greek pine nuts.

TEQUILA: Not just for drinking, this distilled liquor made from the blue agave greatly enhances many recipes. Gold Tequilla, also called "especial" by some manufacturers, obtains its dark rich gold color as it ages in casks that have previously housed other spirits or wine.

TOMATILLOS: Although sometimes called a "green tomato," the tomatillo is a member of a separate family. Native to Mexico and used in a number of southwestern dishes, this small green vegetable with a brown husk has a sharp, acidy taste that lends itself to salsas, chilis, soups, and stews.

Tomatillos are now available in most supermarkets in the Southwest and in specialty food stores and vegetable markets in the rest of the country. You can use canned tomatillos in most recipes but be sure to drain and rinse them well before using.

APPETIZERS

&

STARTERS

MARINA DEL REY HORS D'OEUVRES

I love appetizers and often make a meal of them instead of eating a large dinner. This is one of my favorites. It is not only tasty but has great eye appeal with the mixture of yellow bell pepper, red bell pepper, and green tomatillos and chile served in delicate puff pastry and topped off with a leaf of cilantro and a slice of black olive.

We tried this recipe using purple bell peppers but found that when we cooked them they lost their color and turned a rather dull green, so save them for a dish you don't cook.

1 yellow bell pepper, seeds and membranes removed, thinly sliced

1 red bell pepper, seeds and membranes removed, thinly sliced

6 tomatillos, chopped

1 cup roasted, peeled, seeded, and chopped green chile such as New Mexico Sandia

3 jalapeños, seeds and membranes removed, finely chopped

1 small white onion, finely chopped

1 cup water

2 tablespoons balsamic vinegar

Juice of 1 large lime

1 tablespoon sugar

1 teaspoon salt

1 teaspoon ground allspice

½ teaspoon ground ginger

Puff pastry squares or round tortilla chips

Fat-free cream cheese

GARNISH: *Cilantro leaves, sliced black olives*

Place the bell peppers, tomatillos, chile, jalapeños, onion, water, vinegar, lime juice, sugar, salt, allspice, and ginger in a saucepan and cook over medium heat for 15 minutes. Let cool to room temperature and then refrigerate at least 2 hours before serving.

Just before serving, spread puff pastry squares or tortilla chips with a touch of fat-free cream cheese, top with a spoonful of the chile mixture, and garnish with a sprig of cilantro and a slice of black olive.

Serves 12

SERVING SUGGESTIONS: Serve with cocktails or with an iced herb tea.

ENSENADA BLACK BEAN DIP

I discovered Ensenada in the early 1960s and on several trips was the guest of a marvelous hostess who had traveled the world and was an excellent cook. She put in a standing order every time I returned to California to bring back certain things on the next trip that she couldn't get in Mexico.

As a reward for dutifully running these items down to her, she made some of my favorite treats to go with our evening margaritas—including this dip.

Although you can use different types of chile with the beans, I find the ancho gives this dish an especially enjoyable smoked flavor.

2 tablespoons olive oil

1 small yellow onion, finely chopped

2 cups cooked black beans

1 tablespoon chicken stock

1 tablespoon white wine

1 tablespoon finely chopped fresh cilantro

1 clove garlic, squeezed through a garlic press

1 teaspoon crushed ancho chile

1/2 cup shredded Asadero or Monterey Jack cheese

Juice of 1 large lime

Heat oil in a skillet and sauté the onions until limp. Add black beans and mash with a potato masher until smooth. Add the rest of the ingredients except the cheese and lime juice and simmer until heated through.

Place beans in a shallow bowl. Sprinkle with lime juice, then sprinkle the cheese over the top.

Serves 4–8

SERVING SUGGESTIONS: Serve on a cocktail buffet table with blue corn chips.

BERENJENA CON CHILE ROJO

(Eggplant with Red Chile)

Eggplant and red chile seem to have a natural affinity. This is a wonderfully satisfying first course with its earthy offering of eggplant, garlic, green onions, and olives accented with the zing of red chile.

I'm always amused when certain foods, such as eggplant, evoke such strong emotions. Just the mention of it will make some people shudder and they often say how bitter it is. There are a couple of ways to keep eggplant from having a strong or bitter taste. One is to soak slices of eggplant in salt water, drain and rinse under cold running water, and then pat dry with paper towels. The other is to bake the eggplant in either a conventional oven or a microwave instead of sautéing it (this also reduces the use of fat).

1 medium-size eggplant (approx. 1–1½ lbs.)

½ cup chicken stock or broth

2 cloves garlic, squeezed through a garlic press

3–4 green onions, chopped (including green portions)

2 ribs celery, chopped

2 tablespoons chopped fresh parsley

1 teaspoon chopped fresh cilantro

2 cups peeled and chopped firm, ripe, red tomatoes

1 dried pulla chile pod, crushed with the seeds

¼ cup white wine

¼ cup sliced Greek olives

1 teaspoon freshly ground black pepper

1 teaspoon salt

½ teaspoon allspice

GARNISH: *Lettuce, purple kale or mustard greens, sliced green or black olives, sprigs of cilantro*

Cut the stem end off the eggplant and pierce the large end with the tines of a fork. Place in a microwave-safe dish and microwave on HIGH for 10 minutes or until the eggplant collapses. Remove from the oven and let stand until cool. Peel the skin from the eggplant and cut the flesh into 1-inch cubes.

You can also bake the eggplant in a conventional oven. Prick the skin with a sharp fork and bake at 350 degrees for 30 minutes or until the eggplant collapses and is done inside. When cool enough to handle, peel and cut into cubes.

Simmer the garlic, onion, and celery in the chicken stock for 3 to 4 minutes. Add the cubed eggplant, parsley, cilantro, tomatoes, chile, wine, olives, pepper, salt, and allspice, then cover and cook over low heat until warmed through.

Spoon some of the eggplant mixture on a bed of lettuce or other greens such as purple kale or mustard, and garnish with sliced olives and sprigs of cilantro.

Serves 6–8

SERVING SUGGESTIONS: Served warm as a first course, this makes a fantastic beginning for a pasta dinner. Serve with warm flour tortillas or dark bread squares, accompanied with thin slices of provolone and/or salami. Store any leftovers in the refrigerator and serve cold the next day with crackers.

JALAPEÑOS STUFFED WITH GRILLED TUNA

This is a very popular appetizer in Mexico, often served with drinks in the late afternoon. It is now making inroads into the repertoire of southwestern hosts. I'm passionate about this mixture of freshly grilled tuna integrated with crunchy green onions and carrot, finished off with vermouth redolent of herbs, all housed in fresh, bright, hot red jalapeños. I serve it every chance I get.

8 ounces tuna fillet

3–4 green onions

1 clove garlic

1 small carrot

1 tablespoon fresh parsley

½ teaspoon salt

1 tablespoon fresh lime juice

2 tablespoons dry (French) vermouth

1 tablespoon olive oil

24 red jalapeños, seeds and membranes removed, (you can also use green)

Lettuce leaves

Grill the tuna for 3 minutes on each side or until the fish flakes easily when tested with a fork. Place the onions, garlic, carrot, and parsley in a food processor fitted with a steel chopping blade and process with a few quick pulses.

Break the tuna in pieces, add to the blender, and process with one or two pulses. Add the salt, lime juice, vermouth, and olive oil and process with a few quick pulses until all ingredients are well chopped but not pureed. The mixture should retain the integrity of each ingredient.

Cut the jalapeños in half lengthwise or cut the top third off each chile, leaving the stem on. Scrape out the seeds and remove the membranes. Mound the tuna mixture into the jalapeños. Arrange the jalapeños on a bed of lettuce on a large platter and serve.

Serves 8–10

SERVING SUGGESTIONS: This goes extremely well with margaritas or shots of gold (aged) tequila served in the Mexican manner with salt and lime wedges.

JALAPEÑO ESCABECHE

One of my favorite restaurants serves a bowl of escabeche as soon as you are seated at your table. The colorful marinated vegetables and/or seafood, with blue corn chips, is a great appetizer instead of the ubiquitous salsa served in so many Mexican-style restaurants.

There are as many variations of escabeche as there are cooks, but the most popular one in our household consists of carrots and zucchini, sliced on the diagonal, mixed with pieces of onion, cauliflower, and jícama pickled in a vinegar, garlic, and jalapeño marinade.

You can use either whole or sliced jalapeños. I like to use both red and green varieties. If you can't find the red ones in your market, you can age the green ones yourself. It will take between one and two weeks until they turn a red or a wonderful golden orange color.

3 white onions, each cut into 8 wedges

6 carrots, sliced on the diagonal approx. 1 inch wide

3 medium zucchini, sliced on the diagonal approx. 1 inch wide

1 head of cauliflower, broken into florets

1 medium jícama, peeled and cut into 1-inch strips approx. 1 inch wide

12 cloves garlic, cut in half lengthwise

6 whole jalapeños, stems and membranes removed, cut in half lengthwise (seeded optional)

4 cups white vinegar

1 cup olive oil

4 cups water

½ cup fresh lime juice

1 teaspoon pickling salt or sea salt (regular table salt will cloud the solution)

6 bay leaves, broken in half

2 teaspoons crushed dried oregano

1 tablespoon minced fresh rosemary

8–10 whole cloves

Place the onions, carrots, zucchini, cauliflower, jícama, garlic, and jalapeños in a glass jar or pottery crock. Combine the vinegar, oil, water, lime juice, salt, bay leaves, oregano, rosemary, and cloves in a saucepan and bring to a boil. Pour over the vegetables in the jar. Loosely cover until the contents come to room temperature. Then tightly cover and store in the refrigerator for at least 48 hours before using. Pour the liquid off and remove the bay leaves. Serve the escabeche with tortilla chips or tostadas. It will keep in the refrigerator for up to 2 weeks in the liquid.

Serves 10–12

SERVING SUGGESTIONS: Serve with drinks or as an accompaniment to a southwestern meal. Great with seafood and a real waker-upper with eggs for brunch.

TOSTADAS WITH CARNITAS AND GREEN CHILE

My wife and I thoroughly enjoy taking common ingredients and creating a brand-new dish out of them. This is one of those marvelous dishes that you have to taste; the slightly dry pork, slow-roasted with chile and pepper, then mixed with the unusual combination of spinach, onion, and orange juice served on a tostada will make a believer even out of appetizer haters.

You can either buy tostadas that have been baked or make your own using corn tortillas 3½ inches in diameter.

This recipe uses pork shoulder pieces called carnitas, which can be found in many markets carrying Mexican or South American food products. The pork is cooked on a rack so that most of the fat cooks away and drips into a pan. You can easily make it at home using the following procedure.

FOR THE CARNITAS:

1–1½ pounds pork shoulder

1 teaspoon freshly ground black pepper

1 teaspoon ground mild red chile (such as New Mexico red)

FOR THE TOSTADAS:

½ white onion

2 cloves garlic

½ teaspoon salt

6–8 spinach leaves

1 cup carnitas (reserve the rest for another dish)

1 tablespoon fresh orange juice

3 Anaheim chiles, roasted, peeled, and chopped

½ teaspoon freshly ground black pepper

12 corn tortillas (3½ inches in diameter)

Olive oil for frying

GARNISH: *Whole pitted black olives, marinated artichokes, and sprigs of cilantro*

To make the carnitas: Preheat the oven to 275 degrees. Cut the pork shoulder into cubes approximately 3 x 3 x 2 inches. Rub the pepper and ground red chile into the pork pieces. Place the coated pork on a rack in a baking dish or pan and bake in a 275-degree oven for 4 hours or until the pork has browned and most of the fat has dripped into the bottom of the pan. Discard the fat. Use the pork in the following recipe and in any southwestern recipe calling for carnitas.

To make the tostadas: Place the onion, garlic, salt, spinach, and carnitas in a food processor fitted with a steel blade and chop coarsely. Add orange juice, chopped chiles, and pepper and pulse two or three times just to mix; do not puree. The pork, spinach, and onion should be distinctive entities.

Cover the bottom of a 9-inch frying pan with olive oil and heat until the oil is very hot but does not smoke. Using tongs, dip the tortillas 1 or 2 at a time in the oil. Rapidly fry until lightly brown on both sides. Drain and blot thoroughly on paper towels.

Place 1 to 2 tablespoons of the pork-spinach mixture on the top of each tostada and serve at room temperature, garnished with black olives, marinated artichokes, and sprigs of cilantro. You can also spread a teaspoon of mashed black beans on the tostada, top with the pork mixture, and add a sprinkling of feta cheese for a nice presentation.

Serves 4–6

SERVING SUGGESTIONS: Place 2 tostadas on a salad plate and serve with ice-cold drinks. This also makes a nice starter course for a simple dinner featuring a dish such as Grilled Breast of Chicken with Lemon-Tarragon Marinade (page 157).

 TOSTADAS TOPPED WITH CRAB AND CHILE

The zing of the árbol chile blended with crabmeat, onion, garlic, and cilantro, along with the crunch of raw cashews, makes a splendid appetizer or starter course.

Try making these and two or three other appetizers from this chapter to eat with friends for a leisurely supper or after a movie or play.

1 pound crabmeat

½ small-size white onion

1 clove garlic

1 large firm, ripe tomato

1 árbol chile, seeded and crushed

1 tablespoon fresh lime juice

1 tablespoon olive oil

¼ cup raw cashews

Pinch salt

1 tablespoon chopped fresh cilantro

12 corn tortillas (3½ inches in diameter)

Olive oil for frying

GARNISH: *Cilantro leaves*

Pick over the crabmeat to remove any bone or cartilage. Rinse the meat under cold running water. Place in a small strainer and let drain.

Place the onion, garlic, tomato, and chile in a food processor with a metal blade. Pulse just to chop. Add the lime juice, oil, cashews, salt, cilantro, and crabmeat. Pulse until just blended; do not puree.

Cover the bottom of a 9-inch frying pan with olive oil and heat until very hot but not smoking. Using tongs, dip the tortillas, 1 or 2 at a time, in the oil and rapidly fry until lightly browned on both sides. Drain on paper towels. Spoon the crab mixture on top of each tostada, garnish with a cilantro leaf, and serve at once.

Serves 4–6

SERVING SUGGESTIONS: These go very well with white wine or margaritas.

VERACRUZ VEGETABLE PÂTÉ

We were looking for a starter to begin a sit-down dinner for a client who wanted a vegetarian meal. We didn't want to serve the usual green salad. We came up with this unusual pâté that has the crunch of fresh vegetables and the zing of cayenne.

1 large-size pimento or red bell pepper

1 medium-size carrot, cut into chunks

1 cup broccoli florets

1 medium-size zucchini, stem end cut off, cut into chunks

6 medium-size radishes, cut into quarters

1/2 cup pecans

16 ounces fat-free cream cheese at room temperature

1/2 teaspoon cayenne

1 tablespoon fresh lemon juice

Leaf lettuce

Roast the pimento over an open flame or on a rack in the oven until the skin has blackened and blistered. Remove from oven and wrap in a wet towel and let stand 10 minutes. Then peel off the outer layer of skin and remove the stem and seeds. Place pimento in a food processor with a metal blade. Add the carrot, broccoli, zucchini, radishes, and pecans and chop finely. Add the cream cheese, cayenne, and lemon juice and process until smooth.

Spoon the mixture into a mold or freezer-safe bowl and freeze. Unmold by placing the mold or bowl in a small amount of hot water and gently moving the mold around until the pâté loosens. Turn out onto a plate and carefully slice. To serve, place a lettuce leaf on a salad plate and place a slice of pâté in the center of the lettuce.

Seves 6–8

SERVING SUGGESTIONS: Garnish with carrot sticks, marinated artichoke hearts, and olives, and serve with dark bread or slices of French bread. Or serve this paté with crackers or melba toast for a cocktail party.

RED SNAPPER CEVICHE WITH SERRANO CHILE

Citrus juice "cooks" the seafood in a ceviche. This effective way of preserving the fish originated in Latin America. Fish ceviches are often served in Mexico, but this is one dish that has not traveled as well into the Southwest—perhaps because we are so landlocked. With modern shipping techniques, however, it is easy to get fresh or fresh-frozen fish even in the desert Southwest.

I particularly like red snapper ceviche with a very hot chile such as serrano. Although most traditional Mexican recipes call for using only lime juice, I like to add grapefruit juice to add more depth of citrus flavor to the dish.

For the best ceviche, use only very fresh fish. We have used red snapper for this recipe but shrimp and scallops also make great ceviches.

2 serrano chiles, seeded and chopped

2 pounds red snapper fillets, cut into 1-inch cubes

2 cups fresh lime juice

Juice from 1 medium-size grapefruit

3 green onions, chopped, including green portions

1 tablespoon chopped fresh cilantro

½ teaspoon salt

½ teaspoon ground white pepper

2 large firm, ripe tomatoes, diced

Place all the ingredients except the fish in a glass bowl (do not use metal or plastic) and stir with a wooden spoon or a chopstick. Add the fish and stir, making sure that the fish is covered with the liquid. Cover and marinate in the refrigerator for 8 hours or overnight. Let stand at room temperature for 10 minutes before serving. When ready to serve, drain off most of the liquid.

Serves 6–8

SERVING SUGGESTIONS: Spoon onto lettuce leaves and serve as a first course.

SHRIMP AND JALAPEÑO CEVICHE

I love this recipe since it not only has the delightful taste of shrimp, jalapeño, and tomato but is also simple to prepare and is wonderfully refreshing in the summer.

Select jalapeños that are dark green and firm to the touch. The secret to this dish is to chop the jalapeños very finely. Although you can use a machine to do this, I find that the best and easiest way is to cut the chiles into quarters lengthwise with a sharp knife, scrape out the white membranes and seeds, then line up the strips of chiles and cut them in tiny pieces.

1 pound small shrimp (approx. 36)

2 jalapeños, seeds and membranes removed, finely chopped

1 tablespoon finely chopped white onion

2 medium-size ripe, firm tomatoes, diced

1 tablespoon chopped fresh parsley or cilantro

1 cup fresh lime juice

3 tablespoons fresh lemon juice

Peel and devein the shrimp and wash under cold running water. Place the shrimp in a glass bowl (do not use metal). Add the jalapeños, onion, tomatoes, and parsley, then pour the lime juice and lemon juice over the shrimp and toss lightly. Chill in the refrigerator for at least 8 hours.

Serves 4–6

SERVING SUGGESTIONS: Serve very cold on lettuce leaves. Excellent with a water wafer-type cracker.

# PUMPKIN AND CHORIZO CANAPÉS

This mouthwatering combination of pumpkin and homemade chorizo combines some of the most popular seasonings used in the Southwest. This is excellent served at Thanksgiving time.

Chorizo is a wonderful Mexican-style pork sausage. If you buy it at a supermarket, chances are it will be full of fat. We make our own by grinding turkey breast and very lean pork in a food processor.

FOR THE CHORIZO:

1 tablespoon olive oil

½ small white onion, minced

½ pound ground turkey

¼ pound lean pork loin, ground

1 clove garlic, diced

1 tablespoon New Mexico red chile powder

½ teaspoon ground oregano

½ teaspoon ground cumin

½ teaspoon salt

½ teaspoon freshly ground black pepper

1 tablespoon distilled white vinegar

FOR THE CANAPÉS:

2 cups pumpkin puree (you can use canned unsweetened pumpkin)

24 pastry shells, 2 inches in diameter

GARNISH: *Cilantro leaves*

To make the chorizo: Heat the oil in a frying pan and sauté the onion for 3 to 4 minutes. Add the turkey, pork, and garlic and sauté 3 to 4 more minutes. Add the rest of the ingredients and cook until the meat is lightly browned and crumbly. Pour off any excess fat.

To make the canapés: Mix the pumpkin with the cooked chorizo and heat until warmed through. Spoon into pastry shells and place on heated platter or in a hot chafing dish. Garnish with cilantro leaves and serve warm.

Serves 6–8

SERVING SUGGESTIONS: Serve for a Thanksgiving or Christmas buffet. These go beautifully with hot spiced apple cider.

PICKLED CHILE AND GORGONZOLA EN CROÛTE

Pickled green chile can be used in a number of ways, especially as an appetizer. Spoon it over a block of no-fat cream cheese on a platter surrounded by crackers for a quick and easy no-fuss hors d'oeuvre. Or use it baked with a touch of blue cheese in puff pastry. The latter takes a little more effort but the results are well worth it.

FOR THE PICKLED CHILE:

4 cups diced green chile, such as Anaheim or a New Mexico variety
*   such as Big Jim or Sandia*

1 cup white vinegar

1 cup sugar or fructose

1 tablespoon pickling spice

FOR THE PASTRY:

1 9 x 15-inch sheet of puff pastry

Olive oil

4 ounces Gorgonzola or good blue, Roquefort, or Stilton cheese

Nonstick vegetable spray

To make the pickled chile: Place all the chile ingredients in a saucepan, bring to a boil, reduce heat, and simmer for 10 minutes. Remove from the heat and let cool to room temperature. Use as needed for the following recipe and store the rest in the refrigerator.

To make the pastry squares: Lightly brush the puff pastry with olive oil and cut into 3-inch squares. Crumble some of the cheese over the top of each square, then place a teaspoon or so of the drained pickled chile in the center. Pull up the sheets of dough around the chile and cheese, and pinch together to form a small purse.

Preheat the oven to 400 degrees. Lightly coat a cookie sheet with nonstick vegetable spray. Place each piece on the sheet and bake in a 400-degree oven for 15 minutes or until the pastry has puffed up and is a light golden brown.

Serves 6–8

SERVING SUGGESTIONS: Served piping hot with cocktails, these make a lovely bite just before an elegant dinner party.

CLAMS BAJA

We have always enjoyed the many beautiful beaches in Mexico, especially around the Sea of Cortéz. There are some wonderful small clams to be had in this area and we've found this to be a delightful way to prepare them. Cooking the clams in white wine with a touch of sharp pequín chile gives them a lively, brisk flavor.

FOR THE CLAMS:

1 cup white wine

2 cups water

1 tablespoon crushed pequín chile

3 tablespoons chopped fresh parsley

3 dozen very fresh small clams

FOR THE CHILE BUTTER:

¹/₂ cup butter

¹/₄ cup olive oil

1 teaspoon crushed pequín chile

To cook the clams: Place the wine, water, chile flakes, and parsley in the bottom of a large stockpot and heat to boiling. Add the clams, stir with a wooden spoon, cover, and cook over high heat for 10 to 15 minutes or until the clams open. Discard any that do not open.

To make the chile butter: Place all the ingredients in a saucepan and heat until the butter has melted and the oil is hot.

Serves 2–4

SERVING SUGGESTIONS: Serve the butter in small bowls to dip the clams, along with hunks of sourdough bread or bolillos (Mexican rolls) to sop up any excess chile butter.

ARTICHOKE AND CHILE BRUSCHETTA

With the fresh, clean taste of the artichokes underscored by garlic, cilantro, and the fiery bite of árbol chile, a southwestern cook can make bruschetta his or her own.

The trick to making this dish is to use just enough olive oil to bring the ingredients to a spreadable consistency but not so much that the bread becomes soggy.

1 cup artichoke hearts, drained (for convenience, use canned hearts packed in water)

2 cloves garlic

3 sprigs cilantro

1 tablespoon crushed árbol chile (see Note)

¼ teaspoon salt

½ teaspoon freshly ground black pepper

Juice of 1 lime

Approx. ¼ cup extra-virgin olive oil

1 large loaf of Italian bread

Preheat oven to 400 degrees.

Place all the ingredients, except the olive oil and bread, in a food processor fitted with a metal blade. Chop coarsely. Add the oil a little at a time and process until the mixture becomes spreadable.

Slice the bread into thick slices on the diagonal. Spread the artichoke-chile mixture on one side of each slice. Place on an ungreased baking sheet and bake at 400 degrees for approximately 8 minutes, until the bread is lightly toasted but not hard. Serve at once.

Note: In many stores in the Southwest you can buy crushed árbol and pequín chile, sometimes called "chile flakes" on the package. Or you can crush or grind your own. The traditional way is to use a mortar and pestle, but you can also remove the stem ends of the chile and grind it. I found quite by accident that if you grind the chile in a coffee grinder that contains a slight residue of good coffee, it gives this dish a nice, richly different taste. If you don't want chile-flavored coffee, however, be sure to wash the coffee grinder well after grinding your chile.

Serves 4–6

SERVING SUGGESTIONS: This bruschetta makes a great appetizer with a glass of wine or serves as a starter to a pasta dinner.

SOUPS
&
CHILIS

TORTILLA SOUP

There are as many ways to prepare tortilla soup as there are cooks specializing in southwestern cooking. The debate rages as to whether an authentic tortilla soup has a clear stock base or not, uses tomatoes or not, uses cream or not, and whether the tortillas should be added while the soup is cooking, or placed in the bowl with the hot soup ladled over them.

Here is my version of this southwestern classic using blue corn tortillas.

1 tablespoon olive oil

1 large-size white onion, chopped

1 serrano chile, stemmed, seeded, and chopped

1 clove garlic, minced

2 large firm, ripe tomatoes, peeled, seeded, and quartered

1 tablespoon fresh cilantro

6 cups chicken stock or broth

1/2 teaspoon salt

1/2 teaspoon freshly ground black pepper

2 boneless, skinless chicken breasts (6–8 oz. each), cooked, cut into bite-size pieces

Juice of 1 lime

3–4 blue corn tortillas, cut into strips

1 lime, thinly sliced

Heat the oil in a soup pot and sauté the onion, serrano, and garlic until the onion is tender. Place in a food processor fitted with a metal blade. Add the tomatoes, cilantro, and 2 cups of the chicken stock and blend until smooth. Pour into a saucepan or soup pot, add the rest of the chicken stock, salt, pepper, cooked chicken pieces, and lime juice, cover, and cook over medium heat for 10 minutes.

Ladle the soup into soup bowls, add a few strips of blue corn tortillas to each bowl, top with a slice of lime, and serve.

Serves 4–6

SERVING SUGGESTIONS: This filling soup is perfect as the centerpiece of a meal.

ZESTY LEEK AND POTATO SOUP

The tang of leeks with the earthy freshness of new red potatoes accentuated by jalapeños and red chile is a far cry from standard potato soup. Topped with some feta cheese and cilantro, this is the perfect soup for a sophisticated palate.

If you buy chicken broth for this and other recipes in this book that call for chicken stock, try to find the low-fat broth now available in most supermarkets. If you can't find the low-fat version, pour the broth into a large measuring cup and refrigerate for 2 hours, then skim the fat off the top.

If you're using chicken stock you've made yourself, let it stand overnight in the refrigerator until the fat has congealed on top, then skim it off.

If you are in a hurry, there are a couple of inexpensive new gadgets on the market that let you pour off the chicken stock, trapping the fat behind.

4 medium-size leeks

3 teaspoons salt (divided use)

6 medium-size red potatoes, boiled, peeled, and diced

2 cups chicken stock or broth

4 cups nonfat or low-fat milk

2 jalapeños, seeds and membranes removed, chopped

½ teaspoon ground white pepper

½ teaspoon ground nutmeg

1 teaspoon grated fresh lemon peel

½ teaspoon ground New Mexico red chile

2–3 tablespoons feta cheese

GARNISH: *Sprigs of cilantro*

Trim off the bottoms and tops of the leeks. Open up the leeks and wash carefully. Then cook the leeks in boiling water with 2 teaspoons of salt for 20 minutes or until tender. Drain. Blend the leeks, 2 or 3 batches at a time, in a blender with the potatoes and chicken stock until smooth. Pour into a saucepan, add the milk, jalapeños, pepper, remaining 1 teaspoon salt, nutmeg, and lemon peel and cook over medium heat until warmed through. Ladle into individual soup bowls. Place the red chile powder in the bottom of a small bowl, add the feta cheese, and stir until the cheese is coated with the chile. Sprinkle the chile-coated, crumbled feta cheese over the soup, and garnish with sprigs of cilantro.

Serves 6

SERVING SUGGESTIONS: This makes a lovely first course to an elegant southwestern meal. Follow it with Medallions of Pork with Tepin-Laced Pear Sauce (page 174) or Shrimp Sautéed with Jalapeño and Tequila (page 198).

"CREAM" OF JALAPEÑO SOUP

This soup is a great conversation piece and takes a great many twists and turns with your mouth.

Even though we are trying to eat less fat these days, sometimes good-for-you clear soups are just not satisfying enough and we crave a cream soup. I've discovered that using low-fat canned evaporated milk tastes as good as cream in a soup such as this. Also, the sweet potatoes in this recipe give it an added richness and provide a source of beta carotene.

When using a roux in a recipe such as this, cook the flour in the oil or butter until it just starts to become a very light brown. If you don't brown the roux, the soup will have a floury aftertaste. Be careful, however, not to brown the roux too much or you will be well on your way to making a gumbo.

1 cup water

3 jalapeños, seeds and membranes removed, chopped

1 medium-size yellow onion, finely chopped

1 clove garlic, squeezed through a garlic press

2 tablespoons olive oil or butter

2 tablespoons all-purpose flour

4 cups chicken stock or broth

1 can (12 oz.) low-fat evaporated milk

2 medium-size sweet potatoes, cooked, peeled, and diced

¼ teaspoon ground allspice

½ teaspoon freshly ground black pepper

Pour the water into a medium-size soup pot or saucepan. Add the jalapeños, onion, and garlic and simmer for 5 minutes or until the vegetables are softened. Remove to a bowl and reserve.

Melt the oil or butter in the same pan and stir in the flour to make a roux. Let the roux cook until a very light brown. Then gradually stir in the chicken stock and bring to a boil so that the soup will thicken. Turn the heat down to a simmer and add the reserved vegetables, along with the milk, sweet potatoes, allspice, and pepper. Cook for 10 minutes or until the potatoes are warmed through.

Serves 4 as a main course or 6 as a starter course

SERVING SUGGESTIONS: This is best served with homemade pumpernickel bread. It makes a good starter for a dinner of fish or chicken.

GARLIC SOUP WITH CAYENNE CROUTONS

I learned to make both a stovetop and a baked garlic soup when I lived in Europe. When I started serving the stovetop variety in the Southwest, it got rather ho-hum reviews until my wife suggested we add some chile. Adding the chile directly to the soup didn't seem to work well. Then we hit upon the idea of making cayenne croutons to float on top of the soup, and our friends started sending in rave notices.

Use slender French baguettes to make the croutons. If you can't find baguettes and don't have the time or inclination to make them yourself, substitute a coarse-grained bread cut into rounds, approximately 2½ inches in diameter.

Tip: A handy method for removing the garlic cloves from the husk or shell is to microwave each head of garlic for 30 seconds on HIGH. Then the cloves will pop right out of the shell with no problem.

FOR THE CROUTONS:

1 French baguette, sliced 1 inch thick

2 tablespoons olive oil

1 tablespoon melted butter

1 tablespoon chopped fresh parsley

Juice of ½ lime

Pinch of salt

¼ teaspoon cayenne

½ teaspoon New Mexico red chile powder, such as Big Jim or 6-4

1 tablespoon olive oil

4 whole heads of garlic, separated into cloves and peeled

1 medium-size white onion, peeled and coarsely chopped

6 cups chicken stock or broth

½ cup dry white wine

½ teaspoon freshly ground black pepper

½ teaspoon salt

To make the croutons: Lay the bread slices on an ungreased cookie sheet and let the bread dry out for approximately 1 to 2 hours.

Preheat oven to 350 degrees.

Mix the rest of the crouton ingredients together. Brush or spread a teaspoonful or so onto each slice of bread. Bake in a 350-degree oven for 10 to 15 minutes or until well toasted.

To make the soup: Heat the oil in a heavy saucepan and sauté the garlic and onion until softened. If the pan becomes too dry, add 1 or 2 tablespoons of the chicken stock and continue cooking until the garlic and onion have softened.

Place the garlic and onion in a blender, add 1 cup of chicken stock, and puree. Pour the puree back into the saucepan and enjoy the wonderful aroma while you add the rest of the chicken stock, wine, pepper, and salt. Cook for 10 minutes over low heat.

Ladle into soup bowls and top each with one of the cayenne croutons and serve at once.

Serves 6

SERVING SUGGESTIONS: Serve as a first course with red meat for dinner. Or serve with Mushroom Spinach Salad (page 89) for an interesting luncheon meal.

CHILLED AVOCADO SOUP

This very special soup has a delicate but full flavor, and its velvety sensuousness lingers on the tongue as you enjoy each spoonful.

I've included this in the book because it is a choice soup although avocados have a high fat content; the fat is unsaturated, however. Many of us living in the Southwest would rather have our daily ration of fat by eating an avocado instead of a steak.

1 tablespoon olive oil

½ white onion, finely chopped

4 medium-size ripe avocados, peeled and pitted

1 tablespoon lime juice

½ cup dry white wine

3 cups chicken broth

¼ teaspoon ground white pepper

1 cup nonfat or low-fat milk

¼ teaspoon cayenne

1 tablespoon chopped fresh cilantro

GARNISH: *Chopped fresh chives*

Heat the olive oil and sauté the onions until limp. Place the avocados in a blender, add lime juice, wine, and sautéed onions, and puree. Place the rest of the ingredients (except the chives) in a bowl, stir in the avocado puree, and chill in the refrigerator for at least 2 hours before serving. Ladle into individual bowls, sprinkle with a little chopped fresh chives, and serve.

Serves 4–6

SERVING SUGGESTIONS: Serve at an elegant dinner party followed by a terrine or mousse of salmon, and top the meal off with fresh strawberries with a splash of Grand Marnier for dessert.

CRAB SOUP

This crab soup calls forth the Mexican heritage of the Southwest and incorporates indigenous ingredients—onions, peppers, tomatoes, chile—along with the crab to produce an invigorating soup with layers of flavor.

Tip: Most of us do not have time to make long, involved stocks, so I call for bottled clam juice in this recipe. If you want to make your own fish stock, however, take fish heads and tails (if you have a good rapport with the manager of the fish department in your supermarket, they may give you the fish trimmings at no charge) along with a couple of carrots, 3 or 4 ribs of celery, some chopped onion, a few garlic cloves, 2 or 3 bay leaves, and some fresh herbs such as rosemary, thyme, or marjoram. Add some black peppercorns and a little salt and simmer over medium-low heat for 2 hours. Remove from the heat and let cool, then strain and discard all but the broth.

If you plan on making your own fish stock you can also save fish heads and tails and odds and ends of shellfish such as shrimp shells and freeze until you are ready to use them.

1 medium-size yellow onion, chopped

1 medium-size green bell pepper, seeds and membrane removed, diced

1/4 cup water

2 medium-size ripe, firm tomatoes, peeled and diced

1/2 teaspoon ground cumin

1/2 teaspoon ground oregano

2 bay leaves

6 cups water

1 bottle (12 oz.) clam juice

2 lemons, sliced

1 pasilla chile, stemmed, diced with the seeds

1–1 1/2 pounds cooked crabmeat, picked over and rinsed under cold water

2 cloves garlic, squeezed through a garlic press

1 cup dry white wine

GARNISH: *Sprigs of cilantro*

Simmer the onion and bell pepper in 1/4 cup water until soft. Add the tomatoes, cumin, oregano, bay leaves, 6 cups water, clam juice, lemon slices, and chile, cover, and cook for 30 minutes.

Add the cooked crabmeat, garlic, and wine and cook over medium heat for another 10 minutes. Remove bay leaves and discard. Ladle hot soup into bowls, garnish with a sprig of cilantro, and serve.

Serves 4–6

SERVING SUGGESTIONS: This soup makes a well-rounded lunch meal served with a green salad of curly endive, and crusty sourdough bread.

CRAB, CORN, AND CHILE CHOWDER

This is a colorful soup with its red and green bell pepper, corn, and chile. These ingredients in league with the crab make a soup worthy of the heartiest of appetites.

Tip: The secret to this recipe is good, fresh ingredients. If you have a farmers' market nearby, try to get freshly picked corn and cut the kernels off yourself. It's easy. Remove the husk and the silk from the corn; you may want to run the corn under cold running water to get all the silk off. Then hold the corn vertically over a chopping board and, using a sharp knife, start at the middle of the ear and cut the kernels off using a swift downward motion. Try to get as close to the core of the ear as possible. Then reverse the ear and cut off the rest of the corn.

If you can't get fresh corn, you can use niblets found in the frozen food section of the supermarket.

My preference is yellow corn for this recipe, as white corn has too delicate a flavor to vie with the rest of the ingredients.

1 medium-size onion, chopped

1 large-size red bell pepper, seeds and membranes removed, chopped

1 medium-size green bell pepper, seeds and membranes removed, chopped

1/2 cup water or chicken stock

2 tablespoons olive oil

2 tablespoons all-purpose flour

2 cups chicken stock or broth

4 cups nonfat or low-fat milk

2 cups cooked crabmeat, picked over, rinsed under cold water, and shredded

1 garlic clove, minced

3 cups corn cut from the cob (approx. 6 ears of corn)

4 Anaheim or New Mexico green chiles such as 6-4s or Sandias, roasted, peeled, and diced

1 tablespoon chopped fresh parsley

½ teaspoon salt

1 teaspoon freshly ground black pepper

1 bay leaf

Simmer the chopped onion and bell peppers in ½ cup water or chicken stock until the vegetables are soft.

In a large saucepan or soup pot, heat the oil and add the flour to make a roux. Cook until flour is a light tan color but not brown.

Stir 2 cups chicken stock into the roux and whisk until smooth. Then stir in the milk. Add the rest of the ingredients, cover, and simmer over medium-low heat for 20 minutes.

Remove the bay leaf and serve hot.

Serves 4–6

SERVING SUGGESTIONS: Serve as the main course for lunch with green chile cornbread sticks and guacamole salad.

GAZPACHO

This is my version of the classic Andalusian soup now served throughout Mexico and the Southwest. It is sometimes called a "salad soup" in Spain because it is made with chopped fresh, raw vegetables.

One of my pet peeves is eateries that serve a puree of vegetables that they run through a blender and then label "gazpacho." To me this wonderful soup should only be served with freshly chopped, crunchy vegetables in a tomato, wine, and citrus base.

I will admit that I've taken liberties with the classic form and in addition to bell peppers have added jalapeños to give this gazpacho a nice, piquant flavor. You can add one or two jalapeños, depending on how hot you like the soup.

4 large, very ripe tomatoes, peeled and finely chopped

1 medium-size cucumber, peeled, seeded, and finely chopped

1 medium-size green bell pepper, seeds and membranes removed, finely chopped

1 medium-size red bell pepper, seeds and membranes removed, finely chopped

1 cup finely chopped celery, back strings removed

3–4 green onions, finely chopped with a small amount of the green portion

1 clove garlic, squeezed through a garlic press

1–2 jalapeños, stems, seeds, and membranes removed, finely chopped

2 cups tomato juice (best if fresh)

½ cup dry white wine

½ cup fresh orange juice, strained

1 tablespoon fresh lime juice, strained

½ teaspoon freshly ground black pepper

GARNISH: *Lime slices*

Place all the ingredients, except the lime slices, in a large glass bowl and stir gently. Chill in the refrigerator at least 2 hours before serving. Ladle into soup bowls, garnish with lime slices, and serve.

Serves 4–6

SERVING SUGGESTIONS: Serve on a hot summer day with crusty French or Italian bread.

GAZPACHO VERDE

(Chilled Green Vegetable Soup)

An import from Spain through Mexico, gazpachos vary from cook to cook but usually are red in color, using ripe tomatoes or tomato juice as their base.

In this unusual gazpacho I use green as the key color and chop the tomatillos, cucumber, bell pepper, celery, and onion very fine to preserve the integrity of the vegetables.

The tomatillos used in this recipe have a distinctive flavor. Although they look like small green husked tomatoes, they are actually a member of the Physalis family along with the ground-cherry and Cape gooseberry.

Available in supermarkets throughout the Southwest and in specialty stores in the rest of the country, tomatillos are best used green in sauces and salsas. If you can't find tomatillos you can substitute green tomatoes in this recipe, but the taste is entirely different.

6–8 tomatillos, husks removed, finely chopped

1 medium-size cucumber, peeled, seeded, and finely chopped

1 large-size green bell pepper, seeds and membranes removed, finely chopped

3 ribs celery, back strings removed, finely chopped

4 green onions, finely chopped with some of the green portion

1 jalapeño, seeds and membranes removed, finely diced

1 cup dry white wine

¼ cup fresh lime juice

½ cup fresh orange juice

2 cups water

½ teaspoon ground white pepper

½ teaspoon salt

GARNISH: *Sprigs of cilantro, lime slices*

Mix all the ingredients together, except the garnish, and chill for at least 3 hours in the refrigerator before serving. Serve chilled with springs of cilantro and/or lime slices for garnish. This will not keep; it must be eaten the day you make it.

Serves 4

SERVING SUGGESTIONS: Serve this for lunch on a very hot day with warm flour tortillas or sliced bolillos.

THREE-ALARM ZUCCHINI AND CABBAGE SOUP

Cabbage is the great leveler in soups. It can make the difference between a good vegetable soup and an excellent one. The trick is not to overcook the cabbage, adding it toward the end of the cooking process so that it stays crunchy.

The combination of the manzana and the jalapeño, which are about 5.5 on the heat scale, and the serrano, which is about 7 on the scale, will give this soup not only a great deal of heat but also an unusual and zesty flavor. If you can't find manzanas, which are mostly grown in central Mexico, substitute a poblano, yellow wax, or güero chile grown in California and New Mexico.

1 tablespoon olive oil

1 medium-size yellow onion, chopped

1 pound medium-size zucchini, ends cut off, scrubbed and sliced

*6 cups chicken broth or stock; or beef stock that you have left in the refrigerator
   overnight and skimmed the fat from*

3 medium-size ripe, firm tomatoes, peeled, seeded, and chopped

1/2 medium-size head green cabbage, coarsely chopped

1/2 cup dry white wine

1 serrano chile, roasted, peeled, seeded, and diced

1 manzana chile, roasted, peeled, seeded, and diced

1 jalapeño, finely diced (seeded optional)

1/2 teaspoon ground cumin

1/2 teaspoon salt

1 tablespoon chopped fresh cilantro

Heat the oil in a soup pot and sauté the onion and zucchini until the onion is soft. Add the chicken broth and tomatoes, cover, and cook over medium-high heat for 15 minutes. Add the rest of the ingredients, turn down the heat, cover, and simmer for another 15 minutes or until the cabbage is tender but not mushy. Serve at once.

Serves 4–6

SERVING SUGGESTIONS: Great for a cold day served with heavy dark bread, followed by some Mexican coffee laced with tequila or Kahlua.

CELERY-ALMOND SOUP

Like so many really good recipes, this soup happened by accident. Once, one of my restaurants featured a celery-almond side dish that the customers loved. One morning we had quite a lot left over from the previous night. I needed a soup for a private meeting for businessmen who wanted a quick soup-and-sandwich luncheon. I made some last-minute adjustments to the left-over celery dish and served it as soup. It was such a hit that I went back to the drawing board and created this soup, which we featured from then on.

4 tablespoons olive oil (divided use)

1/2 medium-size yellow onion, finely chopped

4 cups sliced celery, back strings removed

2 tablespoons all-purpose flour

1 cup nonfat or low-fat milk

4 cups chicken broth or stock

1/4 cup dry (French) vermouth

1 teaspoon crushed pequin chile flakes

1/2 teaspoon salt

1/2 teaspoon ground white pepper

1/4 teaspoon ground nutmeg

1/2 cup slivered almonds

GARNISH: *Sliced almonds, sprigs of parsley*

Heat 2 tablespoons of the oil and sauté the onion and celery until the onion is soft and the celery tender. In another saucepan make a roux using the remaining oil and the flour. Stir in the milk and beat with a whisk until smooth, then add the chicken broth, vermouth, chile flakes, salt, pepper, and nutmeg and stir until well blended.

Add the onions and celery and slivered almonds and simmer over low heat until the vegetables are hot.

Ladle into individual bowls and sprinkle a few sliced almonds on the top of each bowl, garnish with a sprig of fresh parsley, and serve.

Serves 4–6

SERVING SUGGESTIONS: Serve as a classy start to a meal of broiled chicken and rice.

POTATO, KALE, AND CHILE SOUP

The combination of potato and kale in soup is very European. This recipe adapts well to the Southwest with the addition of Anaheim chile. I not only like the subtle blend of potato and kale highlighted with the chile but I also love the beautiful, soft green color of the soup as well.

My classic training is in cooking in the French manner where each ingredient is often cooked separately and then combined to finish off a dish. So it was hard for me to learn to do one-pot meals and soups such as the following. Cooking everything in stages in the same pot, however, certainly saves energy, and by not throwing away the water from cooking, you keep more of the vitamins and nutrients.

Just be sure when making the following recipe that the kale is very, very clean before adding it to the soup.

1 medium-size yellow onion, peeled and quartered

6 medium-size white boiling potatoes, peeled and cut into eighths

4 cups water

2 bay leaves, broken in half

1 bunch of green kale, well washed, with the large stem portions cut off

1/2 teaspoon salt

Lemon peel cut in 2 1/2-inch strips

3 large Anaheim chiles, roasted, seeded, and peeled

2 cups chicken stock or broth

1/2 teaspoon freshly ground black pepper

1/4 teaspoon allspice

Place the onion, potatoes, water, and bay leaves in a large soup pot, bring to a boil, then reduce the heat and simmer for 30 minutes. Add the rest of the ingredients, cover, and cook approximately 15 more minutes or until the kale and potatoes are tender.

Remove from the heat and let cool slightly. Remove the bay leaves, then pour the soup a little at a time into a blender and puree.

Return to the soup pot or a saucepan and heat over low heat until warmed through. Serve warm.

Serves 6–8

SERVING SUGGESTIONS: This is excellent served with cornbread or a grilled, sliced chicken breast sandwich on dark bread.

EGGPLANT AND RED CHILE SOUP

The earthy flavor of the eggplant, in concert with ground turkey and typical southwestern spices (oregano, cumin, and allspice), becomes a robust soup when combined with tequila and New Mexico red chile powder.

2 large-size eggplants

2 tablespoons coarse (kosher) salt

1 tablespoon olive oil

1 medium-size yellow onion, chopped

1 pound lean ground turkey

4 cups chicken stock or broth

2 cups water

1/2 cup ground New Mexico mild red chile powder

1 teaspoon dried oregano

1/2 teaspoon ground cumin

1 teaspoon ground allspice

2 cloves garlic, minced

1 tablespoon chopped fresh parsley

1/4 cup gold (aged) tequila

8 ripe tomatoes, peeled and seeded, with their juice (if you can find them, use 4 yellow and 4 red tomatoes)

Peel the eggplant and cut into cubes. Soak the cubes in water to cover with 2 tablespoons coarse salt for 30 minutes. Drain under cold running water and reserve eggplant. Heat the oil in a large soup pot and sauté the onion and ground turkey until the onion is soft and the turkey is lightly browned.

Stir in the rest of the ingredients, cover, and bring to a boil. Reduce the heat and simmer over low heat for 1 hour.

Ladle into individual soup bowls and serve.

Serves 8–10

SERVING SUGGESTIONS: This is a great soup to build a vegetarian meal around. Serve with black bread spread with tahini (sesame-seed paste) and end the meal with fresh fruit.

BLACK BEAN SOUP WITH RED ONION SALSA

The rich, encompassing flavor of black beans with chopped fresh pimentos topped with a salsa made from red onion, garlic, and cilantro produces a deeply satisfying soup.

Although they are mild and we eat them in all sorts of ways (including stuffed in olives), pimentos are a member of the chile family. Pimentos rate about 1 on the heat scale and are especially good when played off against a hotter chile such as ancho.

Note that the secret to the red onion salsa is to use enough salt so that the vegetables do not stick to the sides of the chopper or food processor.

FOR THE SOUP:

1 pound dried black beans

1 medium-size yellow onion, chopped

1 large-size carrot, scrubbed clean and chopped

1 rib celery, chopped

1 whole pimento, roasted, peeled, seeded and chopped

2 cloves garlic, chopped

1/2 teaspoon ground oregano

6 cups water

6 cups chicken stock

1 tablespoon chopped fresh parsley

1/2 teaspoon ground cumin

1 ancho chile, stem removed, finely chopped

FOR THE SALSA:

1 clove garlic, quartered

1 tablespoon finely chopped cilantro

1/2 teaspoon salt

1 red onion, peeled and cut into eighths

1 tablespoon rice wine vinegar

To prepare the soup: Wash and pick over the beans, cover with water and soak overnight. The next day, drain off the water, rinse beans in fresh water, and place in a large soup pot.

Add the rest of the soup ingredients, cover, and bring to a boil. Reduce the heat to low and simmer for 1½ to 2 hours or until the beans are nice and tender.

To prepare the salsa: Chop the garlic and cilantro coarsely in the bowl of a chopper or a food processor fitted with a metal blade. Add the salt, onion, and vinegar and pulse 2 or 3 times to coarsely chop. Do not overchop or blend.

Ladle the soup into bowls and top each serving with a tablespoonful of the salsa.

Serves 8–10

SERVING SUGGESTIONS: Serve with warm flour tortillas and finish the meal with a mango sorbet for dessert. Or use as a first course followed by Red Snapper with Jalapeño and New Mexico Red Chile (page 186).

GREEN CHILE BISQUE

Although the term *bisque* has traditionally referred to a soup made from shellfish and fish broth, the new American cooking has been featuring a host of bisques using other ingredients, including vegetables.

In this unusual, lively blend of onion, celery, green bell peppers, garlic, and serrano and Anaheim chiles, I also eschew the use of cream or egg yolks as a thickener. Instead I puree the vegetables to thicken the bisque. I have clung to one holdover from the old way of making a bisque: adding sherry.

4 tablespoons olive oil (divided use)

1 medium-size white onion, chopped

2 cups chopped celery, back strings removed

1 large-size green bell pepper, seeds and membranes removed, chopped

1 large-size carrot, scrubbed and chopped

1 clove garlic, chopped

2 tablespoons all-purpose flour

2 cups nonfat or low-fat milk

6 cups water

1 bay leaf

2 serrano chiles or 1 habanero chile

1 large-size Anaheim or New Mexico Big Jim chile, roasted, peeled, and seeded

1 teaspoon crushed fresh rosemary

½ teaspoon freshly ground black pepper

½ teaspoon salt

½ cup sherry

Heat 2 tablespoons of the olive oil in a soup pot and sauté the onion, celery, bell pepper, carrot, and garlic for 5 minutes. Reduce the heat, cover, and simmer over low heat for another 10 minutes.

In a separate sauce pan, make a roux with the remaining 2 tablespoons oil and the flour. When the flour is lightly browned, stir in the milk and beat with a whisk until smooth. Add the water, bay leaf, chiles, rosemary, pepper, and salt. Then stir in the sautéed vegetables, cover, and simmer over low heat for 20 minutes.

Let cool slightly and then puree in a blender, a little at a time, until well blended. Return the mixture to the pot, stir in the sherry, and cook over low heat until warmed through.

Serves 4–6

SERVING SUGGESTIONS: This is great for a vegetarian lunch served with blue cornmeal muffins or hearty whole-grain bread. Or use as a first course for a southwestern dinner and follow with Shrimp Sautéed with Jalapeño and Tequila (page 198), topped off with a melon ice or mango sorbet for dessert.

FIESTA POSOLE WITH RED CHILE SAUCE

Posole is a traditional southwestern dish of Indian origin. In New Mexico and Arizona many people feel that Christmas and New Year's celebrations would not be complete without a bowl of posole. Some cooks subscribe to putting red chile in the posole; others make a red chile sauce that is served on the side so that everyone can spoon on the amount of heat desired.

The accepted meat for a posole has always been pork. When we started trying to eat slimmer and lighter and cut down on our red meat intake, however, I experimented with turkey and chicken in the posole. I found that ground turkey works best.

Posole or hominy is available in most supermarkets, especially in the fall around the holidays. In this recipe I also use the liquid the hominy is canned in to give the posole a richer flavor.

The old-guard cooks in New Mexico make this traditional red chile sauce without using any tomato and often use water instead of chicken broth. I find that the chile taste is much more pleasing with the addition of both the tomato sauce and the chicken broth. I've served this a great many times to purists who exclaim how good it is, not knowing that I have broken the rules.

FOR THE POSOLE:

2 tablespoons olive or canola oil

1 large-size onion, chopped

3 cloves garlic, minced

1½ pounds ground turkey breast

1 teaspoon crushed dried oregano

2 teaspoons ground cumin

2 bay leaves

1 cup dry white wine

2 cups water

1 large can (6 lbs., 12 oz.) white hominy, with the liquid

3–4 New Mexico green chiles (such as Big Jim or Sandia), roasted, peeled, seeded, and chopped

1 ancho chile, chopped

FOR THE RED CHILE SAUCE:

3 tablespoons olive oil (divided use)

½ medium-size onion, chopped

2 cloves garlic, minced

2 tablespoons all-purpose flour

1 can (14 oz.) chicken broth

1 small can (8 oz.) tomato sauce

3 tablespoons New Mexico red chile powder

1 teaspoon ground cumin

1 teaspoon salt

To prepare the posole: Heat the oil in a large pot. Sauté the onion, garlic, and turkey, stirring occasionally, until the turkey is cooked through. Stir in the oregano, cumin, and bay leaves. Add the wine, water, hominy, green chile, and the ancho and cook over low heat for at least 1 hour. Remove the bay leaves before serving.

To prepare the red chile sauce: Heat 1 tablespoon of the oil and sauté the onions and garlic until the onions are limp. Heat the remaining 2 tablespoons oil in a heavy frying pan, stir in the flour, and lightly brown to make a roux. Add the chicken broth and stir until smooth. Add the tomato sauce, chile powder, cumin, salt, and garlic-onion mixture. Simmer over very low heat until smooth and well blended. Add more chicken stock or water if necessary to thin the sauce.

Serves 10–12

SERVING SUGGESTIONS: Ladle the posole into bowls and serve with the red chile sauce on the side. This is great for a buffet supper and goes well with guacamole salad and blue corn tortillas.

CHICKEN AND ANASAZI BEAN CHILI

I have served this dish many times and everyone loves the blend of mild New Mexico red chile, basil, oregano, cumin, cilantro, and a jalapeño that expands the mixture of chicken, Anasazi beans, and tomatoes into a dish of superb southwestern taste.

I use 2 tablespoons of mild New Mexico red chile powder in this recipe. If you think this may be too hot for your taste, start with 1 teaspoon and keep adding until you get to the heat level you are comfortable with.

The Anasazi beans I use in this chili are a medium-size cordovan-and-white mottled bean. (To me they look more like a pinto pony than pinto beans do.) They have about the same nutritional value as pinto beans—64 percent carbohydrate, 22 percent protein, 11 percent moisture, 1 percent fat, and 2 percent fiber and minerals. Although they are hard to find in supermarkets, most gourmet shops and health food stores in the Southwest carry them. You can also order them through gourmet mail-order catalogs.

2 tablespoons olive oil

1 medium-size onion, chopped

1 clove garlic, minced

2 tablespoons mild New Mexico red chile powder

1 teaspoon crushed dried basil

1/2 teaspoon ground oregano

1/2 teaspoon ground cumin

1 teaspoon chopped cilantro

4 boneless, skinless chicken breast halves (3 oz. each), cut into cubes

1 jalapeño, seeds and membranes removed, chopped

3 cups chicken broth

1 cup white wine

1 tablespoon Worcestershire sauce

4 cups cooked Anasazi beans, drained

1 cup crushed tomatoes

1/2 teaspoon salt

1/2 teaspoon freshly ground black pepper

Heat the oil in a large, heavy pot and sauté the onion for 3 to 4 minutes. Add the garlic, chile powder, basil, oregano, cumin, and cilantro and stir well. Add the cubed chicken and sauté until lightly browed. Add the jalapeño, chicken broth, wine, Worcestershire sauce, beans, tomatoes, salt, and pepper, then cover and simmer for 1 hour, stirring occasionally.

Serves 4–6

SERVING SUGGESTIONS: The traditional way to serve this is spooned over cooked white rice. Or serve with warm flour tortillas or tortilla chips.

WHITE-ON-WHITE CHILI

White meat turkey and white Great Northern beans form the base for this dish, which features some unusual chili ingredients including yellow crookneck squash along with tomatoes and árbol chile. As well as being a most enjoyable chili in its own right, this is a great way to use leftover turkey.

You can either buy whole árbol chiles or árbol chile flakes, which usually come in small cellophane packages in the Mexican food section of supermarkets in the Southwest. You can also find them in ethnic markets in the rest of the country.

If you buy whole árbols, grind them yourself with a food grinder or chopper. I use the whole chile except for the stem and include the seeds for this recipe.

1 tablespoon olive or canola oil

1 large-size white onion, chopped

2 cloves garlic, finely chopped

4 cups cubed cooked turkey breast

1 teaspoon crushed oregano

1 teaspoon ground allspice

1 tablespoon chopped cilantro

4 cups cooked white Great Northern beans with 2 cups of the cooking water

3 medium-size yellow crookneck squash, scrubbed clean, ends cut off, cubed

4 cups chicken stock or broth

1 teaspoon árbol chile flakes

4 tomatillos, husks and stems removed, chopped

Heat the oil in a large soup pot and sauté the onion and garlic until the onion starts to soften. Add the rest of the ingredients, cover, and simmer over low heat for 30 to 45 minutes.

Serves 4–6

SERVING SUGGESTIONS: Great served with cornbread and a salad of spinach and orange sections dressed with a citrus vinaigrette.

MUSHROOM CHILI

I like finding or inventing unusual chilis such as this one using mushrooms, cannellini beans, red wine, and tepin chile. This is a savory chili that has an earthy, robust taste without using meat.

The tepin chile I use in this recipe registers 8 on the heat scale. However, the heat is not lingering and not cumulative as with some chiles. You get the sensation of heat immediately upon eating the chili, but the heat rapidly fades away, leaving a pleasant flavor in your mouth.

Tip: Some cooks peel mushrooms before using them in a recipe such as this. I feel that scrubbing them with a kitchen brush gets them clean enough. For this recipe I take the stem end out with my fingers and save it to make a vegetable stock for vegetarian soups. Any leftover vegetables will do when making this type of stock: celery tops, celery that has gone too limp to use, carrot tops. You can also add chile stems and seeds if you want your vegetable stock on the warm side.

> 2 tablespoons olive or canola oil
>
> 1 large-size yellow onion, chopped
>
> 2 pounds fresh medium-size mushrooms, scrubbed, with the stem ends removed, sliced
>
> 2 tepin chiles, crushed with the seeds
>
> 2 tablespoons Worchestershire sauce
>
> 1 tablespoon tomato paste
>
> 1/2 cup dry red wine
>
> 1 tablespoon fresh lemon juice
>
> 4 cups cooked cannellini beans with 1 cup of the cooking liquid
>
> 4 cups water
>
> 1 tablespoon chopped fresh parsley
>
> 1/2 teaspoon freshly ground black pepper
>
> 1/2 teaspoon ground allspice
>
> Salt to taste

Heat the oil in a large soup pot and sauté the onion and sliced mushrooms for 5 minutes. Add the rest of the ingredients, cover, and cook over medium heat for 20 minutes or until the flavors have blended. This is one dish in which a taste test is necessary to see if it is ready to go to the table. Add more chiles or more salt and pepper if needed and serve at once.

Serves 4–6

SERVING SUGGESTIONS: This is lovely served with a salad of red oak leaf lettuce, mizuna, and romaine and a semidry white wine.

CHILI BLANCO

Another uncommon ingredient in chili is corn. I think that the shoepeg corn (available fresh in farmers' markets or frozen in most supermarkets) with yellow wax chile, navy beans, and yellow tomatoes creates a chili with many contrasting layers of flavors and a gratifying taste.

I cook the chicken breasts for this recipe in just enough water to cover with 1/2 teaspoon tarragon, some celery tops, and half a dozen black peppercorns. When the chicken breasts are done, remove to a chopping board, and strain the broth into a large measuring cup. Refrigerate the chicken broth for several hours or until the fat comes to the top. Skim the fat off and use the chicken and broth in the following recipe.

1 tablespoon olive or canola oil

1 white onion, chopped

2 cloves garlic, minced

2 cups white shoepeg corn niblets

1 to 2 serrano chiles, stems removed, seeded, and diced

1 yellow Hungarian wax chile, stem removed, seeded and diced

4 cups cubed cooked chicken breasts

1 teaspoon ground white pepper

3 tablespoons fresh lime juice

1 teaspoon salt

1 teaspoon ground cumin

1 teaspoon crushed oregano

4 cups cooked navy or Great Northern beans

1 cup green or yellow tomatoes, peeled and chopped

2 cups defatted chicken broth

4 cups water

Heat the oil in a large soup pot and sauté the onion, garlic, corn, serrano, and yellow wax chile until the onion starts to soften. Add the rest of the ingredients and simmer covered on low heat for 20 minutes or until the flavors are well blended.

Serves 8–10

SERVING SUGGESTIONS: I like to pass rolls baked with rosemary or dill or cornbread with this chili. Top the meal off with Mexican-style flan made with low-fat milk.

LA MESILLA CHILI

Near where we live in New Mexico is a small community that in various times during its life has played host to the Butterfield Stage Line, Geronimo, Billy the Kid, Pat Garrett, and the Confederate Army. Now it hosts thousands of visitors a year while still trying to maintain a certain amount of dignity and serene quality of life for its residents. This chili is named in honor of this noble town.

I still know folks who think that ground beef and kidney beans do a chili make. However, ground turkey has a lot less fat and packs just as much wallop in this chili. I use very ripe or overripe tomatoes in this dish, but you can also use canned tomatoes—do not use canned stewed tomatoes, however.

Every chili cookoff entrant has his or her secret ingredient. My secret weapons for this recipe are a little red wine and a Mexican-style chocolate. The chocolate I use (brand name Ibarra) contains sugar, almonds, cinnamon, and cacao nibs and comes in an octagonal red and yellow box. You can find it or similar products in the Mexican food section of supermarkets or in food specialty stores specializing in Mexican or Latin American products.

This chili is HOT! Reduce the amount of chipotle chile and New Mexico red chile powder if you want to temper the fire.

1 tablespoon olive oil

1 large-size yellow onion, finely chopped

3 cloves garlic, minced

2 pounds ground turkey meat, or diced leftover cooked turkey meat

6–8 large, very ripe tomatoes, peeled and diced; or 3 cups canned whole, peeled tomatoes, chopped

1 or 2 chipotle chiles, stems removed

2–3 tablespoons New Mexico red chile powder

1 triangle (approx. ½ oz.) Mexican-style sweet chocolate

6 cups cooked pinto beans

3 cups water

1 cup dry red wine

1 teaspoon ground cumin

1 teaspoon ground coriander

1 teaspoon ground oregano

½ teaspoon ground cloves

Heat the oil in a heavy pot or Dutch oven and sauté the onion and garlic for 3 to 4 minutes. Stir in the turkey and cook for another 3 to 4 minutes.

Add the rest of the ingredients and bring to a boil. Reduce the heat, cover, and simmer for 1 hour, stirring occasionally.

Serves 8–10

SERVING SUGGESTIONS: Serve this chili with warm flour tortillas and cold beer and follow with a cooling fruit ice or sorbet for dessert.

BLACK BEAN AND CHORIZO CHILI

This is a three-alarm chili, with the chile in the chorizo and the habanero teaming up to make a true chile-head happy.

At 10 on the heat scale, the orange habanero used in this recipe is one of the hottest chiles available. You can use more or less habanero to your taste or you can substitute a milder chile such as red jalapeño. If you use the habanero, my advice would be to use a small amount at first, taste the chili near the end of the cooking process, and then add more if you wish.

1 tablespoon olive oil

1 medium-size yellow onion, chopped

1 medium-size green bell pepper, seeds and membranes removed, chopped

1/2 pound chorizo (see recipe for Pumpkin and Chorizo Canapés, page 26)

2 cloves garlic, squeezed through a garlic press

2 medium-size red potatoes, peeled and diced

3 cups cooked black beans

1/2 orange habanero chile, seeded and chopped

Juice of 1 lime

2 tablespoons chopped fresh cilantro

4 cups chicken stock or broth

Heat the oil in a large saucepan and sauté the onion and bell pepper for 3 to 4 minutes. Stir in the chorizo and cook until lightly browned, then drain off any excess fat. Add the rest of the ingredients, cover, and bring to a boil. Reduce the heat and simmer for 30 minutes.

Serves 4–6

SERVING SUGGESTIONS: Serve with frosty margaritas or very cold "lite" beer and bolillos or crusty French bread. This is a great chili to serve for brunch with scrambled eggs and a Bloody Mary after a late night out with "one too many."

FIVE-PEPPER CHILI

Although a native New Mexican once refused to sell one of my books in her store because I called a chile a "pepper," that is what they are, and like it or not, they are related to the bell pepper.

This recipe calls for one bell pepper and four other peppers or chiles in dried, flaked, powdered, and ground form. It is sure to please dyed-in-the-wool chile aficionados.

1 pound coarsely ground lean sirloin steak

½ cup all-purpose flour

1 teaspoon crushed pequin chile

2 tablespoons olive or canola oil

1 medium-size white onion, chopped

2 tablespoons garlic, squeezed through a garlic press

1 medium-size green bell pepper, seeds and membranes removed, chopped

2 tablespoons ground New Mexico red chile

¼ teaspoon cayenne

1–2 teaspoons crushed chipotle chile

1 tablespoon Worcestershire sauce

1 teaspoon ground cumin

1 teaspoon ground oregano

1 tablespoon chopped fresh parsley

3 cups crushed tomatoes

2 cups beef stock or broth

Cut the steak into cubes. Mix the flour and crushed pequin chile together and dredge the steak in the mixture, coating it well. Heat the oil in a large saucepan and lightly brown the steak. Add the rest of the ingredients, cover, and bring to a boil. Reduce the heat and simmer for 1 hour. I like this served over rice and topped with a few pinto beans.

SERVING SUGGESTIONS: Serve with piña coladas and warm flour tortillas.

BLACK-EYED PEA CHILI

A Texas tradition is that one has to eat black-eyed peas and cornbread on New Year's Day to ensure good luck during the coming year. This is a great way to eat those black-eyed peas any time of the year.

I use a lot of oregano in my soups and chilis. The only oregano I can buy in my area is Mexican oregano. It is milder than Greek oregano, which is commonly sold in most other parts of the country. If you use Mexican oregano, you may want to slightly increase the amount I call for in this recipe.

1 tablespoon olive oil

1 white onion, chopped

2 cloves garlic, squeezed through a garlic press

1 pimento, seeded and diced

1 medium-size sweet potato, peeled and diced

3 tomatoes, peeled and chopped

6 cups cooked black-eyed peas

1 mirasol chile, stemmed and crushed

1 tablespoon tomato paste

3 cups vegetable stock or broth

1 tablespoon chopped fresh basil, or 1 teaspoon crushed dried basil

2 tablespoons ground New Mexico red chile

1/2 teaspoon salt

1 teaspoon freshly ground black pepper

1/2 teaspoon crushed dried oregano

Heat the oil in a large saucepan and sauté the onion, garlic, and pimento until soft. Add the rest of the ingredients, cover, and bring to a boil. Reduce the heat and simmer for 1 hour.

Serves 4–6

SERVING SUGGESTIONS: Serve with blue cornmeal muffins and coleslaw.

GREEN CHILE STEW

Although entitled a "stew," I think of this more as a cross between a soup and a chili, hence I've included it in this chapter. This dish is extremely popular in the Southwest and is featured on the menus of many restaurants. As with any regional dish, there are as many variations as there are chefs. Traditionally a green chile such as Anaheim or New Mexico is used in this recipe. I like to add a small amount of dried jalapeño flakes as well. I use very lean cuts of beef such as round steak and pork loin for this recipe and trim off any visible fat.

1/4 cup all-purpose flour

1 tablespoon dried jalapeño flakes

1 pound lean beef, cut into bite-size pieces

1 pound lean pork, cut into bite-size pieces

2 tablespoons olive or canola oil

1 large-size yellow onion, chopped

2 cloves garlic, minced

2 cups beef stock or bouillon

6 cups water

1 tablespoon tomato paste

3–4 large green chiles such as Anaheim or New Mexico Big Jim, roasted, peeled, and chopped

4 medium-size potatoes, peeled and diced

2 cups yellow corn cut off the cob, or frozen niblets

1/2 teaspoon ground oregano

1/2 teaspoon ground cumin

1 tablespoon chopped fresh parsley

1 teaspoon freshly ground black pepper

1 teaspoon salt

Mix the flour and dried jalapeños together and place in a plastic bag. Add the cubed meat and shake the bag until the meat is coated with the flour mixture. Heat the olive oil in a large soup pot and sauté the meat and onion together until the meat is lightly brown.

Add the garlic, beef stock, and water and cook over medium-high heat for 20 minutes. Add the rest of the ingredients, cover, and simmer over low heat for another 45 minutes or until the meat and potatoes are tender.

Serves 4–6

SERVING SUGGESTIONS: Great served with sourdough bread or cornbread.

SALADS

RADISH, JÍCAMA, AND ORANGE SALAD WITH CHILE DRESSING

The charm of this dish is its sharp contrast of taste and texture. The bite of the radishes along with the sweetness of the orange, coupled with a touch of fire from the pequins, makes this an ideal summertime salad.

FOR THE SALAD:

1 bunch radishes, trimmed and sliced

2 cups jícama, peeled and sliced (see Note)

3 large seedless oranges, peeled and sectioned

6 ounces large, pitted Greek olives, sliced

Lettuce leaves

FOR THE DRESSING:

½ teaspoon sugar

1 teaspoon dry mustard

½ teaspoon salt

1 teaspoon crushed pequin chile

2 tablespoons white wine vinegar

½ cup olive oil

Combine the radishes, jícama, oranges, and olives in a salad bowl. (Note: If you do not use the jícama right away, sprinkle a little lemon juice over it to keep it from turning dark.)

Mix together the sugar, mustard, salt, chile, and vinegar, then slowly whisk in the oil. Pour over the salad, toss lightly, and then place on a bed of lettuce on individual salad plates.

Serves 4

SERVING SUGGESTIONS: You can serve this salad at room temperature or chill in the refrigerator for 30 minutes to 1 hour before serving. This salad makes an excellent accompaniment to chicken with steamed squash or baked potato.

A SALAD OF FUSILLI, SHRIMP, AND VEGETABLES

I particularly like to use fresh seafood including shrimp, crabmeat, tuna, and scallops in combination with pasta. The choices of pasta for salad making are legion. I have found all sorts of shapes, including a pasta in the shape of the state of Texas. Although I call for fusilli in this recipe, you can substitute penne or farfalle or another one of your favorites.

This salad is crunchy and creamy with the bite of pasta cooked *al dente* and the briny taste of shrimp in collaboration with an array of fresh vegetables.

FOR THE SALAD:

8 ounces fusilli, cooked, drained, and cooled

1/2 pound medium shrimp, cooked, peeled, and deveined

2 cups fresh spinach, washed and torn into bite-size pieces

2 medium-size carrots, scrubbed and shredded

3–4 green onions, sliced with a small amount of the green portion

2 cups raw cauliflower florets

FOR THE DRESSING:

1 cup lemon-flavored low-fat yogurt

1/2 cup fat-free sour cream

2 tablespoons dry white wine, or 1 tablespoon white wine vinegar

2 teaspoons Dijon mustard

1 mirasol chile, stem removed, crushed with the seeds

1 tablespoon chopped fresh basil

1/4 teaspoon crushed dried oregano

1/2 teaspoon salt

1/2 teaspoon freshly ground black pepper

2 tablespoons grated Romano cheese (optional)

Place the pasta, shrimp, spinach, shredded carrots, onions, and cauliflower in a salad bowl.

Whisk together the dressing ingredients (except cheese) until smooth. Add a little more wine or a small amount of nonfat or low-fat milk if the dressing is too thick.

Pour the dressing over the salad and toss lightly. Sprinkle Romano cheese over the top of the salad if desired and serve.

Serves 4–6

SERVING SUGGESTIONS: You can serve this salad at room temperature or chill in the refrigerator for 30 minutes to 1 hour. Serve this in a bowl with some crusty French or Italian bread for a casual luncheon. Or place leaf lettuce on a plate and mound the salad in the center, and garnish with some tomato wedges or yellow plum tomatoes.

GREEN CHILE FETTUCCINE SALAD WITH BASIL-CHILE DRESSING

I was thrilled when pasta became one of the "in" things to eat. I particularly like using unusual pastas in salads—especially a fettuccine made with green chile or jalapeños.

This is a distinctive salad with layers of chile flavor alternating with the soft texture and mild taste of the artichoke hearts and the crunch of the cucumber and red bell pepper.

You can buy chile-flavored pastas in the gourmet section of your supermarket, specialty food stores, and through mail-order catalogs. When using a chile-flavored pasta I try to use a chile in the dressing that will complement the pasta. For this salad I use a green chile pasta and a medium-hot green chile such as New Mexico Sandia in the dressing; if you like a spicier taste, use a serrano in the dressing.

FOR THE SALAD:

12 ounces green chile fettuccine, each length cut into 4 pieces, cooked according to package directions, cooled to room temperature

2 cups artichoke hearts packed in water, drained

2 medium-size cucumbers, peeled, seeded, and chopped

1 large-size red bell pepper, seeds and membranes removed, sliced

FOR THE DRESSING:

2 tablespoons fresh lime juice

2 tablespoons balsamic vinegar

1½ cups fresh basil leaves, washed

1 clove garlic, quartered

*2 medium-size New Mexico green chiles, such as Sandia, or 1 serrano chile,
    roasted, peeled, and seeded*

½ teaspoon freshly ground black pepper

¼ teaspoon salt

¼ cup olive oil

Place the fettuccine, artichoke hearts, cucumbers, and bell peppers in a salad bowl. Put the lime juice, vinegar, basil, garlic, chile, pepper, and salt in a blender or food processor fitted with a steel blade and blend until smooth. With the processor running, slowly add the oil and blend until smooth.

Pour the dressing over the pasta, toss lightly, and serve.

Serves 4–6

SERVING SUGGESTIONS: You can serve this salad at room temperature or make ahead and chill, covered, in the refrigerator for 1 hour. This makes a nice light supper served with garlic toast or lemon muffins and a chilled glass of medium-dry white wine.

AVOCADOS STUFFED WITH SHRIMP PEQUÍN

The appeal of this salad is its layers of flavors and textures: chilled shrimp, the crunch of celery and cashews, the hint of zesty pequín-flavored dressing, and then the soft, ripe avocado.

Although you can buy cooked shrimp, I prefer cooking my own as they usually taste fresher and I can season the cooking water in order to give an added zip to the finished dish.

To cook the shrimp yourself put 2 bay leaves, half a dozen black peppercorns, 1/2 lemon cut in two, some celery tops, and a tablespoon of dried parsley in approximately 4 cups of water and bring to a boil. Add the shrimp to the water and cook for 2 to 3 minutes or until the shrimp turn pink. Do not overcook or the shrimp will be tough. Drain the shrimp and let cool, then peel and devein.

FOR THE SALAD:

l pound shrimp, cooked, peeled, deveined, each shrimp cut into 3 or 4 pieces, covered and chilled in the refrigerator for 1 hour

2 ribs of celery with the strings removed, chopped

3–4 green onions, chopped with a small amount of the green portion

FOR THE DRESSING:

1 teaspoon chopped fresh chives

1 tablespoon chopped fresh parsley

1/2 teaspoon crushed pequín chile

2 teaspoons white wine vinegar

2 tablespoons olive oil

1/2 cup chopped raw cashews

1/2 teaspoon freshly ground black pepper

3 large-size avocados

Lemon juice

GARNISH: *Sprigs of parsley*

Place the cold shrimp with the celery and onions in a medium-size mixing bowl. Mix together the chives, parsley, chile, vinegar, and oil and stir. Pour the vinegar and oil mixture over the shrimp mixture, add the cashews and pepper, and lightly toss.

Cut the avocados in half, peel, and remove the pits and sprinkle a little lemon juice over them. Spoon the shrimp mixture into the center of each avocado half, garnish with parsley, and serve at once.

Serves 6

SERVING SUGGESTIONS: Arrange kale or lettuce leaves on glass plates, place the avocado halves on top of the lettuce, and serve with blue cornmeal muffins for a luncheon dish.

CRAB COMPUESTA SALAD

Katy Griggs, the owner of the famed La Posta restaurant in New Mexico, claimed to have invented tostadas compuestas in 1939. The chefs at this famous southwestern eatery fried corn tortilla cups and filled them with chile con carne and beans, then topped them with shredded lettuce, diced fresh tomato, and grated yellow cheese.

For many years everyone followed suit—deep-frying a corn tortilla and filling it with pinto beans, sometimes refried, and with chile Colorado (pork in a red chile sauce).

Lately, however, cooks are using all sorts of ingredients in compuestas. Instead of frying the corn tortilla, I discovered that you can make the cups in the microwave without using any fat.

Using that technique and filling the cups with a delicate blend of crabmeat, celery, peas, and cucumber—accented with the smoky taste of cascabel chile—is an example of what some chefs and food critics are calling the "new" southwestern cuisine.

FOR THE SALAD:

4 very fresh corn tortillas (5 inches in diameter)

3/4 pound crabmeat, cooked, picked over, rinsed, and shredded

3 ribs of celery with the back strings removed, finely chopped

3–4 green onions, chopped with a small amount of the green portion

1/2 cup small green peas, cooked, drained, and chilled

1 small-size cucumber, peeled, seeded, and chopped

FOR THE DRESSING:

1 tablespoon fresh lime juice

1 tablespoon fresh orange juice

2 tablespoons fat-free yogurt

1 cascabel chile, stem removed, chopped

1 tablespoon chopped fresh parsley

½ teaspoon ground white pepper

GARNISH: *¼ cup grated carrot; black olives*

Shape the tortillas over a small microwave-safe glass bowl to make a basket or cup, and cook one at a time on HIGH in a microwave for 1 minute. Remove from microwave and let stand for 4 to 5 minutes; it will crisp up as it sits.

Place the crabmeat in a mixing bowl and add the celery, onions, peas, and cucumber. Mix together the dressing ingredients. Stir the dressing into the crab mixture, and lightly mix.

Fill the tortilla cups with the crab mixture, sprinkle a few shreds of grated carrot over the top, and stick 2 or 3 olives into the sides of the salad.

Serves 4

SERVING SUGGESTIONS: Place the compuestas on lettuce leaves and serve for a special lunch with frosty margaritas.

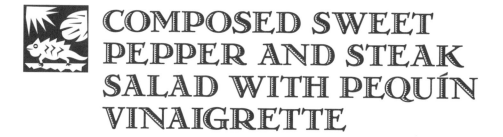

COMPOSED SWEET PEPPER AND STEAK SALAD WITH PEQUÍN VINAIGRETTE

Although I now eat very little red meat, I still get a craving every so often for a good steak. In this simple salad I get the taste and pleasure of red meat without eating as much as sitting down to a full steak dinner.

The sliced filet mignon with the bell peppers and onions, topped with the tang of the pequín vinaigrette, makes for a rich-tasting salad.

Most vinaigrettes call for oil. I use olive oil, but I try to use the least amount possible. Instead of trying to always find a fat replacement, I reduce the amount of oil in the recipe and then use common sense when spooning the dressing on my salad. Now I use a couple of teaspoons instead of a couple of tablespoons.

In this dressing I use club soda to give volume instead of using more oil. The club soda, along with the rich, fiery taste of the pequín, gives this dressing a real kick.

One trick I've discovered: Rather than dress the salad in the kitchen before serving, invest in some pretty sauce boats and bring the salad to the table with the dressing on the side. Let the diners help themselves so that each person can control how much dressing to use.

FOR THE SALAD:

2 filet mignons (4–6 oz. each)
1 head of leaf lettuce, washed, leaves separated
1 large-size red bell pepper, seeds and membranes removed, sliced into rings
1 large-size yellow bell pepper, seeds and membranes removed, sliced into rings
1 medium-size red onion, very thinly sliced
Grated Romano cheese (optional)

FOR THE PEQUÍN VINAIGRETTE:

1 tablespoon Dijon mustard
3 tablespoons balsamic vinegar
2 teaspoons crushed pequín chile
1/2 medium-size white onion, quartered
1 clove garlic
1 teaspoon crushed dried oregano
1/4 teaspoon salt
1/4 teaspoon freshly ground black pepper
1 tablespoon olive oil
1/2 cup club soda

To make the salad: Grill the steak just until very rare, then let cool to room temperature. Refrigerate for at least 2 hours. Slice tissue-thin and reserve.

Place leaves of lettuce on individual plates, then arrange the rings of bell pepper and slices of filet mignon over the lettuce. Top with the onion and pour the pequín vinaigrette over the salad. Grate a small amount of Romano cheese over the top if desired and serve at once.

To make the pequín vinaigrette: Place all the ingredients except the oil in a food processor fitted with a steel blade and process. Scrape down the bowl with a rubber spatula, turn on the machine again, and add the oil in a slow stream through the feeder opening in the top. Process until well blended, then stir in the club soda.

Dressing yield: Approx. 3/4 cup

Serves 4

SERVING SUGGESTIONS: This salad is nice served with toasted bagels. Top the meal off with a mango ice cream or mango cobbler for a great southwestern lunch or light dinner.

The pequín vinaigrette is not only great on this salad but is also good on large mixed green salads, corn salads, or mixed bean salads.

CUCUMBER AND CHILE SALAD

As a child, whenever I visited my maternal grandmother in the summer, the dining room table always held a cut-glass bowl of sliced cucumbers, swimming in a mixture of vinegar, sugar, and salt. In the days before air conditioning they were very refreshing. I find that a variation of this salad using hot chile seems just as cooling on a hot southwestern summer afternoon.

2 large-size cucumbers, peeled and cut into ⅛-inch slices

¼ cup white wine vinegar

1 tablespoon sugar

2 teaspoons coarse (kosher) salt

1 red serrano chile, stem removed, finely chopped

Place the cucumbers in a glass bowl. Stir together the vinegar, sugar, salt, and chile and pour over the cucumbers. Chill in the refrigerator for at least 1 hour before serving.

Serves 4–6

SERVING SUGGESTIONS: Serve with a light, flaky white fish such as halibut or perch.

WILD RICE AND ASPARAGUS SALAD WITH CHIPOTLE DRESSING

We are lucky enough to have friends who live in wild-rice country in Minnesota and bring us a year's supply each time they visit. This salad came about one day when I thought a tabbouleh salad would be nice but didn't have any bulgur wheat in the kitchen. It also seemed appropriate since I was experimenting with some wheat-free recipes for a friend who is allergic to wheat. This midwestern/southwestern tabbouleh salad has since become one of his—and our—favorites.

Very thin asparagus is essential to this dish. Asparagus grows wild in many parts of the Southwest and is best picked while still pencil-thin.

FOR THE SALAD:

1 cup raw wild rice

1 large ripe, red tomato, seeded and diced

2 green onions, chopped with some of the green portion

1 tablespoon capers, drained

1/2 teaspoon salt

1/2 teaspoon freshly ground black pepper

1 tablespoon fresh lemon juice

1 tablespoon fresh lime juice

1 tablespoon olive oil

Lettuce leaves

12 cooked, thin asparagus spears

FOR THE CHIPOTLE DRESSING:

1 red bell pepper, roasted and peeled, seeds removed

1 cup fat-free yogurt

1 chipotle chile, stem removed

Pinch of salt

Let the wild rice stand in cold water to cover for 1 hour, then drain and repeat the process at least once more. Place the drained rice in a pan, cover with water, cover pan, and cook for 1 hour or until tender. Let cool to room temperature.

Place the rice in a glass salad bowl. Add the rest of the salad ingredients, except the lettuce and asparagus, and toss lightly. Chill in the refrigerator for at least 1 hour.

To make the dressing: Place the red bell pepper, yogurt, chipotle, and salt in a food processor or blender and blend until smooth.

Place lettuce leaves on 4 individual salad plates, spoon some of the wild rice salad onto the lettuce, place 3 cooked asparagus spears over the rice, and top with a dollop of the dressing.

Serves 4

SERVING SUGGESTIONS: This salad will make an excellent starter course for a seafood dinner, or serve it with broiled steak.

FARFALLE AND SCALLOP SALAD WITH CITRUS VINAIGRETTE

Eating this salad comprised of scallops, watercress, arugula, and farfalle (bow-tie pasta) mentally transports me to a deck overlooking the Mediterranean.

The citrus used in the dressing is a wonderful counterpoint to the jalapeño. Citrus fruit also makes great salad dressings, and I find that using citrus juice instead of vinegar means that the amount of oil can usually be reduced.

FOR THE CITRUS VINAIGRETTE:

1 orange, ends cut off, quartered

1 poblano chile, seeded and quartered (see Note #1)

Juice of 1 fresh pink grapefruit (approx. 3/4 cup)

1/2 cup honey

1/2 teaspoon salt

1/2 teaspoon freshly ground black pepper

1 tablespoon chopped fresh cilantro

1 jalapeño, seeds and membranes removed, diced (see Note #2)

1 teaspoon crushed fresh rosemary

2 teaspoons olive oil

FOR THE SALAD:

1 cup dry white wine

1 pound small bay scallops

1 bunch of watercress, hard stems cut off, washed well

2 tablespoons chopped fresh parsley

1 bunch arugula, washed and torn into bite-size pieces

*4 cups cooked farfalle, prepared according to package directions and chilled in
    the refrigerator*

To make the vinaigrette: Process the orange, with the peel, in a food processor fitted with a steel blade until chopped. Add the poblano and chop. Add the rest of the dressing ingredients and blend.

Note #1: For this recipe I do not roast and peel the poblano. When it is chopped in the food processor it is not tough. It also gives the vinaigrette a fresh, lively taste. However, this dressing will not keep—you have to use it immediately. You can roast and peel the poblano before using. Although it will still be good, it does change the taste and texture of the dressing.

Note #2: I do not seed the jalapeño in this recipe. Southwestern folklore has it that the seeds are good for your digestion. The seeds do make the dish hotter, however, and you can seed the jalapeño if you wish.

To make the salad: Pour ¼ of the vinaigrette into a medium saucepan, add the wine and scallops, and poach over medium heat until the scallops turn white and are resistant to the touch. Drain and let cool, then slice.

Place the watercress, parsley, arugula, and farfelle in a salad bowl and add the sliced scallops. Pour the rest of the vinaigrette over the salad and toss lightly.

Serves 4–6

SERVING SUGGESTIONS: Serve this salad as part of a buffet lunch, or mound the salad on curly lettuce on individual plates. This is also nice served with a cranberry-nut or pumpernickel bread.

CORN, ZUCCHINI, AND TOMATO SALAD WITH PEQUÍN VINAIGRETTE

We consider corn a staple in the Southwest and eat a great deal of it. Fresh corn, zucchini, tomatoes, and arugula—chilled and accented with a pequín vinaigrette in which mustard and orange juice play a major role—are especially refreshing on a dry, hot southwestern day.

If you are using fresh corn for this recipe, remove the husk and the cornsilk, drop the ears into boiling water and blanch for 2 minutes, drain, and plunge into cold water to stop the cooking process. Let the corn stand for a few more minutes, then cut the kernels off the cob with a sharp knife. Or use defrosted frozen corn niblets.

I call for pequín in this salad dressing because it is one of my favorite red chiles. I love the distinct flavor of the pequín, although the heat rating of this chile is from 7 to 8, which is hot! If you like your chile even hotter, you may substitute árbol, which is slightly hotter than the pequín, or tepin, which is hotter still!

FOR THE SALAD:

1 cup white corn kernels (approx. 2 ears)

3 cups yellow corn kernels (approx. 6 ears)

2 medium-size zucchini, ends cut off, scrubbed clean, scored vertically with a fork, and sliced on the diagonal

2 large ripe, red tomatoes, peeled, seeded, and diced

2 cups (approx.) arugula, washed and torn into bite-size pieces

2 fresh pimentos or red bell peppers seeded and cut into julienne strips

1 cup chopped fresh parsley

1 medium-size red onion, diced into squares approx. the same size as the kernels of corn

FOR THE PEQUÍN VINAIGRETTE:

¼ cup white wine vinegar

½ cup fresh orange juice

1 tablespoon Dijon mustard

2 teaspoons dried, crushed pequín, árbol, or tepin chile

1 clove garlic, quartered

1 teaspoon ground coriander

¼ teaspoon salt

¼ teaspoon freshly ground black pepper

1 tablespoon olive oil

To make the salad: Place all the ingredients for the salad in a salad bowl and chill in the refrigerator for 1 hour. Then lightly toss with the dressing and serve.

To prepare the pequín vinaigrette: Place all the ingredients for the dressing in a food processor fitted with a steel blade and process. Scrape down the bowl with a rubber spatula, turn on the machine again, and process until well blended.

Dressing yield: Approx. 1 cup

Serves 4–6

SERVING SUGGESTIONS: This salad makes a nice vegetarian lunch with whole-wheat rolls. This salad also travels well.

The vinaigrette used for this salad is also good with mixed green salad, tomato and onion salad, or garbanzo bean salad. You can also cut down the amount of mayonnaise you would ordinarily use for a potato or pasta salad by mixing this vinaigrette half and half with the mayonnaise.

HEARTS OF PALM WITH CUCUMBER-CHIPOTLE DRESSING

Hearts of palm used to appear on the menus of chic eateries across the country. I still enjoy them—especially as I find that they make a great vehicle for a chile dressing.

Tossed with spinach, mustard leaves, yellow tomatoes, and prosciutto and topped with a smoky chipotle dressing, hearts of palm provide the basis for an elegant salad to start or finish a sit-down dinner.

The combination of the smoky chipotle chile, combined with fresh cucumber and heady anchovy paste, gives the dressing for this salad an intriguing complex blend of flavors.

FOR THE DRESSING:

1 large-size cucumber, peeled and seeded

1/2 cup drained, cooked garbanzo beans

1/2 cup fat-free yogurt

1/2 teaspoon crushed chipotle chile (see Note)

1 1/2 teaspoons chopped fresh oregano, or 1/2 teaspoon crushed dried oregano

1 teaspoon anchovy paste

1/8 teaspoon ground cumin

1 teaspoon freshly grated ginger

FOR THE SALAD:

12–16 large spinach leaves, well washed and dried

4–5 curly mustard leaves

1 can (14.4 oz.) whole hearts of palms, drained

8–12 yellow plum tomatoes, cut in half

8 thin slices prosciutto

Shredded carrot

To make the dressing: Place all the dressing ingredients in a food processor and blend until smooth. Let stand at room temperature while you prepare the salad.

Note: Although the traditional way to crush chipotle chile was with a mortar and pestle, it's a lot easier to crush the dried chipotle in a food processor fitted with a steel blade or in a coffee grinder. Store any leftover ground chile in a small glass jar with a tight lid for future use.

To make the salad: Place the spinach and mustard leaves on 4 individual salad plates. Divide the hearts of palm equally on the plates. Arrange the plum tomatoes and slices of prosciutto around the hearts of palm. Top with a little shredded carrot. Pour the cucumber-chipotle dressing over the salad and toss lightly.

Dressing yield: Approx. 1¼ cups

Serves 4

SERVING SUGGESTIONS: Serve as the starter course for an elegant dinner such as tournedos or roast capon. Also nice as an upscale note to end a late-night supper of broiled chicken, or Chicken and Anasazi Bean Chili (page 52) or White-on-White Chili (page 53). The cucumber-chipotle dressing is also good as a sauce with grilled salmon or as a dipping sauce for chilled shrimp.

SALPICÓN WITH ÁRBOL CHILE DRESSING

The English translation of *salpicón* is "salmagundi," which is a salad-like mixed dish of chopped meat or poultry or fish with onions and oil. This is my version of a traditional Mexican dish that is popular throughout the Southwest for a summer luncheon or as one of the dishes on a festive buffet table.

The most popular meat for this dish is cooked brisket. Since brisket contains a lot of fat, you might want to use a leaner cut of beef such as round steak.

If using brisket, have the butcher trim off the fat, then trim it again at home. I like cooking the brisket for a long time in a slow oven. One way to do this is to place the well-trimmed brisket in a pan, mix 1 tablespoon of either crushed árbol or pequín chile or 2 tablespoons of New Mexico red chile powder with inexpensive champagne or white wine and pour over the meat. Cover tightly with aluminum foil and place in an oven set at 250 degrees. Cook the brisket 8 hours or overnight. This slow cooking helps melt away the fat. Remove the brisket from the liquid in the pan and let cool to room temperature, then refrigerate overnight. Scrape off any fat you can see and then use the meat in the following recipe.

FOR THE SALAD:

2 pounds brisket or other roast beef, cooked and shredded

6 green onions, chopped with the green portion

Leaf lettuce

Wedges of ripe tomatoes
Sliced green pimento-stuffed olives

FOR THE DRESSING:

2 tablespoons olive oil

3 tablespoons red wine vinegar

1 tablespoon lemon juice

1 clove garlic, squeezed through a garlic press

1 teaspoon crushed árbol or pequín chile

1 teaspoon chopped fresh cilantro

½ teaspoon salt

½ teaspoon freshly ground black pepper

Place the beef and onions in a salad bowl, preferably glass.

In a separate bowl, mix the dressing ingredients. Pour the dressing over the meat and onions and toss lightly. Place the meat on a bed of lettuce leaves, arrange tomato wedges around the edge of the plate, sprinkle the sliced olives on top of the meat and serve.

Serves 6–8

SERVING SUGGESTIONS: Great served with warm, soft corn or flour tortillas and very cold Mexican beer such as Tecate or Corona.

 # APPLE, JÍCAMA, AND CHICKEN SALAD

For this recipe, I use tart apples that have a lot of crunch, such as Cortlands or Winesaps. I avoid apples labeled "delicious" as they are usually soft and mushy and do not hold up in a salad.

Although jícama is somewhat similar in texture to the apples, when the two are combined with chicken, chile, and pecans, the result is a bright-tasting, hot, and sweet salad for a picnic or a summer luncheon dish.

2 boneless, skinless chicken breasts (approx. 8 oz. each)

½ teaspoon crushed pequín or árbol chile

1 cup white wine

1 cup chicken stock or broth

3 tart apples

1 medium-size jícama, peeled and diced

¼ cup lemon juice

2 jalapeños, seeds and membranes removed, chopped

1 cup pecan halves

2 tablespoons chopped fresh parsley

½ teaspoon ground allspice

¼ teaspoon ground cardamom

½ teaspoon salt

½ teaspoon freshly ground black pepper

3 tablespoons fat-free yogurt

1 tablespoon mesquite honey

Curly lettuce leaves

GARNISH: *Red, yellow, or purple bell pepper rings and jalapeño rings*

Rinse the chicken under cold running water and trim away any excess fat and membranes. Place the chicken in a heavy frying pan with the crushed chile, wine, and chicken stock, cover, and poach over medium heat for 20 minutes or until the chicken is done. Drain and let the chicken cool, then dice. (Reserve the stock and add to your soup pot—the crushed chile will give your soup a great zing.)

Core and dice the apples with the skin on. Place the apples and jícama in a salad bowl, pour the lemon juice over them, and stir to coat. Add the jalapeños, pecans, parsley, allspice, cardamom, salt, pepper, yogurt, honey, and chicken and mix well.

Spoon the salad onto lettuce leaves and place bell pepper rings on top of the salad with a jalapeño ring inside each bell pepper ring.

Serves 4–6

SERVING SUGGESTIONS: Serve with a dry white wine and hot sourdough rolls.

GRILLED PINEAPPLE AND CHICKEN SALAD WITH ADOBO DRESSING

This warm salad with its vibrant colors will put some excitement into a meal for a summer evening or a garden party. It is easy to prepare on a charcoal or gas barbecue.

Some people find cutting fresh pineapple rings a daunting experience. The trick to peeling the pineapple is to wear gloves, hold the pineapple upright by the spines, and cut away the skin with a sharp knife. Cut straight down deep enough to get rid of the embedded pieces and continue with straight-down cuts around the entire pineapple. Then cut off the top and bottom and it becomes an easy job to slice the fruit. Then use a paring knife to cut out the woody center pieces.

When choosing the kohlrabi for this recipe, try to find the smallest ones, which are the sweetest. Larger ones have a tendency to be tough and woody.

My wife, Guylyn Morris Nusom, uses fruit such as grapes to add body and flavor to salad dressings. This dressing with its mildly hot adobo flavor clings to the chicken-pineapple mixture and makes a remarkably simple salad into a real triumph.

FOR THE SALAD:

3 skinless, boneless chicken breast halves (approx. 4 oz. each)

½ cup fresh lime juice

¼ cup gold (aged) tequila

½ teaspoon crushed pequin chile

1 clove garlic, squeezed through a garlic press

8 fresh pineapple rings, approx. ½ inch thick

4 large leaves of purple kale

8 lettuce leaves

2 medium kohlrabi, peeled and sliced

Garnish: 4 green onions, including green portion, cut in half lengthwise

FOR THE DRESSING:

2 tablespoons Adobo Sauce (see Breasts of Chicken with Adobo Sauce, page 167)

1 cup fat-free yogurt

24 large seedless green grapes

Trim any excess fat and membranes from the chicken and rinse under cold water. Slice the chicken in strips approximately ¼ inch thick and place in a glass bowl.

In a separate bowl, mix together the lime juice, tequila, chile, and garlic and pour over the chicken. Cover and refrigerate for 2 hours.

Remove from the refrigerator and let come to room temperature (approximately 30 minutes).

To make the dressing: Place all the dressing ingredients in a food processor fitted with a steel blade and blend until smooth and pale orange in color.

To serve: On each of 4 large salad plates or small dinner plates, arrange a leaf of purple kale and two leaves of lettuce.

Heat a griddle made of a heavy metal such as cast iron on an open fire or stove burner. When hot, grill the chicken strips and pineapple rings until the chicken is done and the pineapple has browned. This will happen very rapidly—from 3 to 5 minutes depending on how hot your fire is.

When the chicken and pineapple are done, place 2 rings of pineapple on each plate of lettuce leaves, and arrange the chicken strips and kohlrabi over the pineapple. Spoon a tablespoonful of the adobo dressing over the top. Garnish the plate with half a green onion on each side and serve.

Dressing yield: Approx. 2 cups

Serves 4

SERVING SUGGESTIONS: This is great served at a patio party. Give everyone a tall cold drink such as gold tequila, cranberry juice, and club soda and serve this warm salad with flour tortillas that have been steamed with white wine.

The adobo dressing is also nice served with a shrimp and avocado salad or as an accompaniment to grilled chicken or fish.

LAYERED CABBAGE, POTATO, PIMENTO, AND ARUGULA SALAD WITH FIERY VINAIGRETTE

Mention potato salad and most of us envision a large, soggy mound of potatoes with a few bits of green poking through a heavy white dressing. This salad will immediately dispel that image. Layered on an attractive platter, this makes a great presentation for a buffet or a picnic and you won't have to worry about the mayonnaise running or going bad on a hot summer day.

I love the taste of cabbage and potatoes together and this salad shows off that combination to its best advantage.

This salad dressing is not for the faint of heart. The combination of the tepin and habanero will heat up an entire room. If you would like less heat you can cut down the quantities, or substitute a milder chile such as a pequín for the tepín and a cascabel for the habanero.

FOR THE SALAD:

6 medium-size red-skinned new potatoes

2 bay leaves

1 small head of cabbage

1 large red onion, thinly sliced

2 fresh pimentos or red bell peppers, seeded and thinly sliced

3 ribs celery, back strings removed, sliced

2 tablespoons chopped celery leaves

2 tablespoons chopped fresh cilantro

½ bunch of arugula, washed and torn into bite-size pieces

FOR THE FIERY VINAIGRETTE:

1 tepín chile, crushed

¼ habanero chile, finely diced

Juice of 1 lime

¼ cup white wine vinegar

2 tablespoons olive oil

½ cup club soda or seltzer water (see Note)

1 clove garlic, minced

1 tablespoon crushed fresh rosemary, or 1 teaspoon crushed dried rosemary

½ teaspoon ground mustard seed

½ teaspoon salt

To make the salad: Boil or steam the potatoes in water to cover with the 2 bay leaves until the potatoes are tender but not mushy. Drain; discard the bay leaves. Let potatoes cool, then slice them with the skins on.

Shred the cabbage and blanch or steam in salted water for 3 to 4 minutes. Drain and dry. Cover an oval platter with the cabbage. Arrange the sliced potatoes on top of the cabbage, overlapping each slice.

Next add the slices of onion, pimento, and celery. Sprinkle the celery leaves, cilantro, and arugula around the edge. Serve with the fiery vinaigrette on the side.

To make the dressing: Place all the dressing ingredients in a food processor fitted with a steel blade and blend until smooth.

Note: Using club soda or seltzer in a vinaigrette lightens it, so you can use less oil than you normally would.

Dressing yield: Approx. 1 cup

Serves 4–6

SERVING SUGGESTIONS: This is a great salad to accompany oven-baked chicken. Serve with corn-on-the-cob and top off the meal with watermelon slices or Papaya Salsa (page 109). The fiery vinaigrette is also good with a cold asparagus salad or wonderful over a combined citrus salad.

BELGIAN ENDIVE AND ORANGE SALAD WITH MANGO VINAIGRETTE

Endive is so delicate that any dressing you use needs to be on the mild side. My favorite topping for an endive salad used to be walnut oil, but since I wanted to use pecans in this recipe I developed a dressing that did not use oil.

The mango provides a wonderful flavor for the dressing, and the cayenne gives the salad a zing but does not overpower the endive.

FOR THE MANGO VINAIGRETTE:

1½ teaspoons white wine vinegar

2 tablespoons fresh lime juice

1 cup diced mango

1 tablespoon honey

½ teaspoon freshly ground black pepper

⅛ teaspoon ground cayenne pepper

⅛ teaspoon salt

FOR THE SALAD:

1 head purple kale, washed

4 Belgian endive, washed, with the leaves separated

2 large seedless oranges, peeled and sectioned

½ cup pecan halves

To make the vinaigrette: Place all the vinaigrette ingredients in a blender and blend until smooth. Let stand at room temperature while you prepare the salad.

To make the salad: Place a couple of leaves of kale on each of 4 individual salad plates. Equally divide the endive and oranges on each plate, sprinkle pecans on top, and add a spoonful of mango vinaigrette.

Dressing yield: Approx. 1¼ cups

Serves 4

SERVING SUGGESTIONS: This is a marvelous accompaniment for shrimp dishes. I like to serve it with Shrimp Sautéed with Jalapeño and Tequila (page 198). It's also nice as a first course for a light beef dinner or with grilled fish.

The mango vinaigrette is also good as a marinade with broiled or baked chicken, or brushed on a bruschetta for a different first course or hors d'oeuvre.

SALMON SALAD WITH YOGURT-DILL DRESSING

If you're planning an elegant dinner party and feel like you're swimming upstream and don't have time to do everything, this salad is easy, particularly since you don't have to cook the salmon and can often buy it already sliced.

The New Mexico chile I like to use in this recipe was named after Roy Nakayama, who was with the Agricultural Department at New Mexico State University for many years and developed several strains of chile. If you can't find the R. Naky chile, you can substitute one of the other New Mexico green chiles on the market or you can use Anaheim.

FOR THE SALAD:

Kale or a curly green leaf lettuce

1/2 pound smoked salmon, thinly sliced

1 cup artichoke hearts, packed in water, drained

2 medium-size pink grapefruit, peeled and sectioned

FOR THE YOGURT-DILL DRESSING:

1 cup fat-free yogurt

1 clove garlic, squeezed through a garlic press

1 teaspoon chopped fresh dillweed

1 tablespoon chopped fresh parsley

1 New Mexican green chile such as R. Naky, roasted, peeled, seeded, and diced

Arrange the kale or lettuce on individual salad plates and arrange the salmon, artichoke hearts, and grapefruit on the lettuce.

Mix together the dressing ingredients, spoon over the salad, and serve.

Serves 4

SERVING SUGGESTIONS: Serve with sliced dill boule (a round loaf of French bread) and chilled vodka for an after-theater supper.

SUMMER SALAD GREENS WITH SUN-DRIED TOMATO VINAIGRETTE

There is nothing quite as southwestern as sun-dried tomatoes. The people of the Southwest have been drying them for centuries, first on the flat adobe roofs, then on the tin roofs that topped the adobe structures. We even have a friend who places the tomatoes on a tray, covers them with a screen, and drives them around in her Volkswagen until the heat inside the car dries them.

The salad that plays host to this earthy vinaigrette uses the bounty of fresh greens that come to us in the early summer. I like to use a wide variety of different greens in this salad, including one or two of the soft-leaf lettuces such as oak leaf or Bibb, spinach, arugula, watercress, and some basil and/or mint leaves.

The secret to using the sun-dried tomatoes in this recipe is to put them in a plastic bag and freeze them for 10 to 15 minutes to make them easier to chop or crumble into the salad dressing.

FOR THE SALAD:

Any combination of the following greens and leaves to serve 4–6 people: oak leaf lettuce, Bibb lettuce, radicchio, watercress, arugula, romaine, spinach, mint leaves, and basil leaves

FOR THE SUN-DRIED TOMATO VINAIGRETTE:

2 tablespoons white wine vinegar

2 tablespoons fresh lemon juice

2 tablespoons chopped fresh parsley

1/4 teaspoon crushed árbol chile

1/2 teaspoon salt

1/2 teaspoon freshly ground black pepper

1 clove garlic, quartered

6–8 sun-dried tomato slices that have been frozen for 10–15 minutes, then diced or crumbled

1/2 cup olive oil

To make the salad: Wash the greens you are using and tear them into bite-size pieces. Reserve.

To make the vinaigrette: Combine all the ingredients and let sit in a glass container for at least 1 hour to develop the flavor.

Pour the vinaigrette over the assorted greens, toss lightly, and serve at once.

Serves 4–6

SERVING SUGGESTIONS: This is a great salad for almost any occasion. Use it as a side dish for soy burgers (or the real thing) or grilled meat or fish.

CHILLED CAULIFLOWER AND PIÑON NUT SALAD

I developed this salad one evening in late summer in New Mexico. The temperature had soared to over 100 and the afternoon rain had made the air unusually sultry.

I had bought a wonderful-looking cauliflower that day at the local farmers' market but couldn't bear the thought of eating it hot on such a sweltering day.

The bite of the piñon nuts in concert with the heat of both the New Mexico red and pequín chile and the chilled cauliflower made me forget the tropic-like atmosphere of the day.

Piñon nuts or pine nuts are common throughout the Southwest; the piñon tree is the state tree of New Mexico. The nuts are harvested in the northern part of both New Mexico and Arizona.

The hard seed coat is difficult to remove. New Mexico schoolchildren take great delight in cracking the nuts with their teeth—especially when the teacher's attention is turned toward the blackboard. The nuts are used in many southwestern dishes including muffins and candy, and ground as a coating for chicken and fish.

1 medium-size head of cauliflower

3 tablespoons chopped fresh parsley

¼ cup shelled piñon nuts

½ teaspoon freshly ground black pepper

1 teaspoon ground New Mexico red chile

1 tablespoon olive oil

¼ cup white wine vinegar

1 teaspoon crushed pequín chile

Break the cauliflower into florets, wash, and cook in salted water to cover until just barely tender. Do not overcook. Drain and put into a glass salad bowl. Mix the remaining ingredients together, pour over the cauliflower, toss gently, and chill before serving.

Serves 4–6

SERVING SUGGESTIONS: Serve this salad with roast turkey, or Roast Rack of Lamb with Orange-Pequín Sauce (page 183).

MIXED GREEN SALAD WITH PIÑON AND GREEN CHILE DRESSING

Nothing could be more southwestern or excite the palate more than the combination of piñon nuts and green chile. To add a tasty zest to the salad, I've added pickled ginger. You can buy this sweet/sour product in Japanese markets.

FOR THE SALAD:

A combination of romaine, leaf, red leaf, and iceberg lettuce for 4–6 people—washed, dried, and torn into bite-size pieces

12–14 large mushrooms, washed and sliced

3–4 green onions, chopped with the green portions

FOR THE PIÑON AND GREEN CHILE DRESSING:

½ cup fresh orange juice

1 tablespoon fresh lemon juice

½ garlic clove, squeezed through a garlic press

2 tablespoons chopped New Mexico green chile, roasted, peeled, and seeded

1 teaspoon minced pickled ginger

1 tablespoon olive oil

¼ teaspoon salt

¼ teaspoon ground oregano

¼ teaspoon ground coriander

¼ teaspoon freshly ground black pepper

½ cup shelled piñon nuts

Place greens, mushrooms, and onions in a salad bowl. Mix the dressing ingredients, except the nuts, together. Pour over the salad and toss lightly. Sprinkle the piñon nuts on top and serve.

Serves 4–6

SERVING SUGGESTIONS: Serve with grilled lamb or trout.

MUSHROOM-SPINACH SALAD

I used to think I had to drench a spinach salad in hot bacon fat in order to eat it. After I mended my wicked fat-eating ways, I discovered that a salad such as this one with fruit and mushrooms, topped off with a zesty jalapeño-laced dressing, was the best way ever to eat a spinach salad.

FOR THE SALAD:

1/2 pound fresh button mushrooms, washed and sliced

1/2 pound fresh spinach, washed, dried, stems removed, torn into bite-size pieces

3 green onions, chopped with the green portion

3 tangerines, peeled, sectioned, seeded

FOR THE DRESSING:

1/4 cup olive oil

Juice of 1/2 lemon

1 clove garlic, squeezed through a garlic press

1 jalapeño, minced

1/4 teaspoon dry mustard

1/4 teaspoon salt

1/2 teaspoon freshly ground black pepper

Place the mushrooms, spinach, onions, and tangerine sections in a salad bowl. Mix together the dressing ingredients. Pour over the salad and lightly toss. Serve at once.

Serves 4–6

SERVING SUGGESTIONS: This is a nice salad for a change of pace in a holiday meal. It complements roast meat or poultry and is great with bruschetta.

GARBANZO BEAN SALAD

Garbanzo beans, introduced to the New World by the Spaniards, are grown in several states in Mexico and have long been a favorite in southwestern cooking.

This salad with its rustic, earthy flavor is simple and easy to prepare. It also keeps and travels well so it is perfect for a picnic.

1 tablespoon olive oil

1 tablespoon red wine vinegar

1 tablespoon fresh lemon juice

2 cloves garlic, minced

1 large-size red onion, thinly sliced

2 large-size tomatoes, coarsely chopped

1 pimento or red bell pepper, chopped

1 jalapeño, seeds and membranes removed, chopped

3 tablespoons chopped fresh parsley

⅛ teaspoon cayenne pepper

4 cups of freshly cooked garbanzo beans, drained; or 2 (15 oz.) cans garbanzo beans, drained and rinsed under cold running water

Mix all the ingredients together and chill in the refrigerator at least 2 hours before serving.

Serves 6–8

SERVING SUGGESTIONS: My favorite way to serve this salad is with some sliced cheese and crusty sourdough bread.

SALSAS, SAUCES, & CONDIMENTS

INTRODUCTION

Salsas—which is Spanish for sauce—are the cornerstone of southwestern cooking.

To many people salsa is the hot tomato-and-chile dip served with corn tortilla chips when they sit down to a meal in a Mexican restaurant. But salsas go far beyond that. They offer infinite combinations of tastes, textures, and colors to liven any meal. You can use a wide array of ingredients in making salsas. Although most of the salsas in this book use chile, many excellent salsas come to the table with no chile in them.

Salsas with chile run from mild to hot. And although the matter of whether a salsa is truly hot can often be subjective, I advise everyone making salsas to experiment with the chile, adding a little first and then adding more to achieve the heat factor they and their guests and family are comfortable with.

The more citrus juice or high-acidity vinegar you use, the longer the salsa will keep. Salsas without citrus juice or ones that use a mild vinegar should be eaten right away.

My recommendation for the salsas in this book is that they be kept, in the refrigerator, for no longer than two to three days unless otherwise noted in the recipe.

In the past, fat has traditionally given us many of the intense flavors we so enjoy. Now that people are cooking and eating lighter, salsas are one low-fat way to infuse great flavor into our food and make it tasty and exciting.

The following salsas and sauces can be used in a variety of ways—as dipping sauce for crackers, tortilla chips, and crudités, or as marinades and accompaniments to a wide assortment of meat and vegetable dishes. I have noted in each recipe some of the various ways to use them, but try them with all sorts of food. Be adventuresome in your cooking and the rewards will be in the wondrous taste sensations you can achieve.

CUCUMBER-MANGO SALSA

Like so many really good recipes, this salsa came about quite by accident. I was hosting a television show and had planned to prepare a mango salsa that did not call for cucumber.

Somehow a cup of diced cucumber from another segment of the show found its way onto the tray of ingredients. Since I don't work with a script or a TelePrompTer, I blithely added the cucumber thinking it must belong. The result was so good that I'm passing this simple salsa on to you.

The audience at the show ate this salsa with blue corn tortilla chips. I have also served it with grilled shrimp and it was more than delicious.

2 cups chopped fresh mango

1 cup diced, seeded cucumber

1/2 medium-size white onion, chopped

3 tablespoons fresh lime juice

1 tablespoon chopped fresh cilantro

1/2 teaspoon crushed pequin chile

Mix all the ingredients together and refrigerate for at least 1 hour before serving.

Yield: Approx. 1 1/2 cups

SERVING SUGGESTIONS: This fresh-tasting salsa goes well with broiled or grilled fish such as red snapper.

MANGO SALSA

This sweet/hot salsa with its taste of fresh mango and the bite of jalapeño is super served in the summer. Mangoes, similar to a peach in flavor but not in texture, grow well in Mexico. With their ripe, fragrant, tropical flavor they are a favorite with southwestern cooks.

2 cups chopped fresh mango

2 cloves garlic, squeezed through a garlic press

1 jalapeño, seeds and membranes removed, finely chopped

½ teaspoon salt

½ teaspoon ground white pepper

¼ cup fresh lime juice

Mix all the ingredients together and refrigerate until ready to use.

Yield: Approx. 2½ cups

SERVING SUGGESTIONS: Serve with grilled tuna or sliced roast pork or blue corn chips.

SAN JUAN SALSA

The sweetness of the pineapple in tandem with the red tomatoes, green New Mexico chile, and the dried ancho chile creates a delightful salsa with a full, rounded flavor.

1 tablespoon olive oil

1 large red onion, chopped

2 cups peeled and chopped tomatoes

2 New Mexico green chiles such as Big Jim, roasted, peeled, and chopped

1 ancho chile, seeded and chopped

1 cup diced fresh pineapple, or canned unsweetened pineapple

1/4 cup fresh lime juice

1 teaspoon ground cumin

1 teaspoon chopped fresh cilantro

1/2 teaspoon salt

1/2 teaspoon freshly ground black pepper

Pinch ground nutmeg

Heat the oil in a saucepan and sauté the onion until translucent. Stir in the rest of the ingredients and simmer over very low heat for 15 minutes. Chill in the refrigerator before serving.

Yield: Approx. 3 1/2 cups

SERVING SUGGESTIONS: This is a great accompaniment to grilled swordfish or shrimp.

SUMMER SALSA

I like shopping at the local farmers' market for just-picked, sweet, juicy, ripe melons that I can blend with fresh out-of-the-field chile and pineapple for a salsa that tastes like summer.

1 medium-size cantaloupe, peeled, seeded, and diced

1 medium-size honeydew melon, peeled, seeded, and diced

1 medium-size pineapple, peeled and diced

Juice of 3–4 limes

2–3 yellow wax chiles, seeded and finely diced

1 tablespoon finely chopped fresh cilantro

½ teaspoon ground ginger

¼ teaspoon salt

Combine all the ingredients and refrigerate at least 3 hours before serving.

Yield: Approx. 6 cups

SERVING SUGGESTIONS: I like to serve this on a buffet where I have a lot of cold meats and sliced cheeses. It also goes well with baked or grilled chicken.

TOMATO-CILANTRO SALSA

The taste of fresh cilantro, red tomatoes, tomatillos, and jalapeños gives a truly southwestern flair to this dish. This is my version of the classic Mexican salsa.

8 large ripe tomatoes, peeled and chopped

4 tomatillos, peeled and chopped

1 medium-size yellow onion, chopped

3 Anaheim or New Mexico green chiles, such as Big Jim or 6-4, roasted, peeled, and chopped (seeded optional)

1 jalapeño, membranes removed and chopped (seeded optional)

2 cloves garlic, squeezed through a garlic press

3 tablespoons white vinegar

1 tablespoon chopped fresh cilantro

1/2 teaspoon freshly ground black pepper

1/4 teaspoon crushed oregano

Mix all the ingredients together and refrigerate for at least 1 hour before serving.

Yield: Approx. 3 cups

SERVING SUGGESTIONS: Good as a dip with chips or with grilled vegetables. Although it is also good served with all sorts of meat and egg dishes, I like to serve this salsa with just a few baked corn chips.

GREEN TOMATO SALSA

This salsa lives up to the old saying, "Necessity is the mother of invention." I had to have a salsa recipe for a demonstration, the tomatoes on my vines weren't ripe, and I didn't have time to dash to the store. I used the green tomatoes, added jalapeños, cilantro, and some hot-pepper sauce, served it with baked tortilla chips, and everybody loved it.

1 medium-size onion, diced

2 cloves garlic, minced

6–8 medium-size green tomatoes, diced

2 medium-size ripe tomatoes, diced

2 jalapeños, seeds and membranes removed, chopped

1 tablespoon chopped fresh cilantro

½ teaspoon salt

3–4 dashes Tabasco® sauce

Juice of 1 lime

Juice of 1 lemon

Mix all the ingredients together and refrigerate until ready to use.

Yield: Approx. 2 cups

SERVING SUGGESTIONS: Serve as a dip with blue corn tortilla chips, or try spooning a little on top of hot vegetarian lasagna.

JALAPEÑO SALSA

The fresh flavor and sharp bite of jalapeño married to green bell pepper, tomatoes, plus a touch of Mexican-style chocolate—made with cinnamon, ground almonds, and granulated sugar—makes a dynamic salsa that will electrify any party.

This salsa is HOT, HOT, HOT! If you want to modify the heat, reduce the number of jalapeños.

12 jalapeño peppers, seeds and membranes removed, diced

3 large-size green bell peppers, seeds and membranes removed, diced

1 can (15 oz.) whole peeled tomatoes (including liquid), chopped

2 medium-size onions, diced

2 cloves garlic, minced

½ teaspoon salt

½ teaspoon freshly ground black pepper

1 teaspoon ground cumin

½ teaspoon ground ginger

½ teaspoon grated Mexican chocolate

Mix all the ingredients together and refrigerate for 1 hour before serving.

Yield: Approx. 3 cups

SERVING SUGGESTIONS: Serve as a party dip with crudités or broiled chicken.

# A CLASSIC SALSA

The classic method of preparing this salsa in a Mexican household is to put all the ingredients on a large chopping board and cut them into each other, dicing and turning, dicing and turning, then scrape into a bowl and serve.

To me there is no better taste than the freshness of the avocado combined with the jalapeño, tomato, and cilantro.

1 large-size slightly firm avocado, diced

1 large firm tomato, diced

1 jalapeño, seeds and membranes removed, diced

1/2 medium-size white onion, diced

Pinch salt

1 tablespoon lemon juice

1 teaspoon cilantro

Mix all the ingredients together and serve at once. Plan ahead to use it all, as this salsa will not keep.

Yield: Approx. 1 cup

SERVING SUGGESTIONS: Great accompaniment for grilled red snapper or chicken tacos.

TRICOLOR SALSA

Since the Mexican flag is red, green, and white, I try to find a dish that embodies those colors every year for my Cinco de Mayo (Mexican Independence Day) party. One year I did tricolor enchiladas, one year tricolor tamales.

This past year I came up with this tricolor salsa. Although I used a yellow bell pepper as I couldn't find a white one, it tasted so good no one even noticed.

1 large-size red bell pepper, seeds and membranes removed, diced

1 large-size green bell pepper, seeds and membranes removed, diced

1 large-size yellow bell pepper, seeds and membranes removed, diced

2 cups peeled and diced tomatoes

1 medium-size white onion, diced

½ teaspoon salt

½ teaspoon freshly ground black pepper

1 tablespoon chopped fresh cilantro

Juice of 1 lime

Mix all the ingredients together. Refrigerate for 1 hour before serving.

Yield: Approx. 2 cups

SERVING SUGGESTIONS: Serve with roast meat, fajitas, or tortilla chips.

WATERMELON SALSA

When the Fourth of July approaches and I start planning our Independence Day celebration, I always think of watermelon. I grew tired of serving it as a dessert or salad, so I came up with this salsa, which is very refreshing on a hot July afternoon.

2 cups diced, seeded watermelon

1 cup diced honeydew melon

1 cup peeled and diced jicama

1 Anaheim or New Mexico green chile, roasted, peeled, and chopped

1 tablespoon fresh lime juice

2 tablespoons fresh chopped cilantro

Mix all the ingredients together and refrigerate for 1 hour before serving. This salsa will not keep well for more than a day.

Yield: Approx. 3 cups

SERVING SUGGESTIONS: Serve with baked salmon or sautéed shrimp.

APRICOT SALSA

The color and texture of the combined apricots, pineapple, avocado, and red bell pepper make an impressive and tasty salsa.

1 cup diced fresh apricots

½ medium-size pineapple, peeled and diced

¼ medium-size white onion, diced

1 large-size avocado, peeled, pitted, and diced

1 medium-size red bell pepper, seeds and membranes removed, diced

2 tablespoons fresh lime juice

1 tablespoon chopped fresh cilantro

½ teaspoon salt

½ teaspoon freshly ground black pepper

Combine all the ingredients, toss lightly, and refrigerate for 30 minutes before serving.

Yield: Approx. 3 cups

SERVING SUGGESTIONS: This makes a splendid accompaniment to roast pork or lamb.

CHRISTMAS SALSA

I love the combination of cranberry with a green chile such as jalapeño. I use the whole orange, including the skin, in this recipe, which is a variation on old-fashioned holiday cranberry relish. It stands out in my mind because I was always the one elected in our family to hand-grind the fruit in the days before food processors.

The whole orange along with some wonderful dried apricots and the subtle mix of ginger, cilantro, and cinnamon gives this salsa a bright, fresh taste.

2 medium-size navel oranges, whole, with the ends cut off

1 pound whole cranberries, washed well

2 jalapeños, seeds and membranes removed, chopped

¼ cup chopped dried apricots

1 tablespoon fresh cilantro

½ teaspoon ground cinnamon

¼ teaspoon ground allspice

¼ teaspoon ground ginger

Place the oranges, skin and all, in a food processor fitted with a steel blade and chop very fine. Then add the cranberries, jalapeños, apricots, and the spices and process again. Do not overchop as you want to retain the integrity of the cranberries, apricot, and jalapeño.

Refrigerate for at least 1 hour before serving.

Yield: Approx. 4 cups

SERVING SUGGESTIONS: This is marvelous with roast turkey, and I often use it on an English muffin as a substitute for marmalade.

PICKLED GINGER SALSA

I'm mad for pickled ginger and for pickled chile—so why not combine the wonderful tastes of the two!

3 medium-size red bell peppers, seeds and membranes removed, diced

6 medium-size green bell peppers, seeds and membranes removed, diced

2 medium-size white onions, diced

1 cup water

6 Anaheim green chiles, roasted, peeled, seeded, and diced

1 cup white wine vinegar

1/4 cup peeled and grated or thinly sliced gingerroot

1/2 cup sugar

1 teaspoon salt

1 teaspoon ground allspice

Place peppers, onions, and water in a microwave-safe bowl and cook on HIGH in a microwave for 1 to 2 minutes or until vegetables are tender.

Add the green chile, vinegar, gingerroot, sugar, salt, and allspice. Cook uncovered in the microwave on HIGH for 2 to 3 minutes.

Let cool to room temperature and serve. Store any leftovers in the refrigerator.

Note: If you do not have a microwave, you can steam the peppers and onions for 5 to 6 minutes, then add the rest of the ingredients and simmer, uncovered, over low heat for 8 to 10 minutes or until the sugar dissolves.

Yield: Approx. 6 cups

SERVING SUGGESTIONS: This salsa is particularly good with grilled chicken and rice or served with a block of fat-free cream cheese, crackers, and fresh fruit as a unique dessert.

EGGPLANT SALSA

The intriguing, almost exotic texture of the eggplant, mixed with the pungent balsamic vinegar, cheese, and pequín chile, is a laudable salsa.

1 medium-size eggplant

1 tablespoon water

1 clove garlic, squeezed through a garlic press

2 tablespoons balsamic vinegar

1 tablespoon fresh lemon juice

¼ cup freshly grated Parmesan cheese

1 tablespoon chopped fresh parsley or cilantro

½ teaspoon crushed pequín chile

Cut the stem off the eggplant, cut in half, then place cut side down on a microwave-safe plate with 1 tablespoon water. Cover with plastic wrap and microwave on HIGH for 5 minutes or until tender.

Let cool, then peel and dice the eggplant. Place in a bowl with the rest of the ingredients, mix well, and refrigerate for 1 hour before serving.

Note: If you do not have a microwave, you can prick several holes in the eggplant with the tines of a fork and bake in a 350-degree oven for 30 minutes. Let cool, then peel and chop.

Yield: Approx. 2 cups

SERVING SUGGESTIONS: Serve with blue corn tortilla chips or crackers. Or use as a side dish for baked rack of lamb, or serve with hummus, falafel, and tabbouleh for a vegetarian buffet.

PARTY SALSA

The mixture of the fresh tomatoes with the tomatillos, New Mexico green chile, jalapeño, cilantro, and oregano creates an epic salsa to serve when you have a crowd over.

6 medium-size ripe, red tomatoes, peeled and chopped

3 tomatillos, chopped

1 medium-size white onion, diced

3 New Mexico green chiles, such as Big Jim or Sandia, roasted, peeled, and seeded

1 jalapeño, seeds and membranes removed, finely diced

2 cloves garlic, squeezed through a garlic press

3 tablespoons red wine vinegar

2 teaspoons minced fresh cilantro

1 teaspoon freshly ground black pepper

½ teaspoon salt

½ teaspoon crushed dried oregano

Mix all the ingredients together and refrigerate for 1 hour before serving.

Yield: Approx. 3 cups

SERVING SUGGESTIONS: Serve with tortilla chips or as a side dish with grilled steaks or chicken.

SHRIMP, GRAPEFRUIT, AND AVOCADO SALSA

Salsas are generally thought to be made from vegetables or fruit, but I like to add the unexpected—like shrimp—to my salsas. The grapefruit, avocado, shrimp, and the wonderful tang of the red jalapeño make for an uplifting culinary experience. I use ground dried shrimp, which can be found in Mexican or Asian food markets.

  2 tablespoons ground dried shrimp

  ½ cup fresh pink grapefruit juice

  2 tablespoons fresh lime juice

  1 red jalapeño, membranes removed and finely diced (seeded optional)

  1 cup finely diced celery, back strings removed

  1–2 medium-size green onions, chopped, white portion only

  2 medium-size avocados, peeled and sliced

  2 teaspoons grated grapefruit peel

  ¼ teaspoon freshly ground black pepper

  ½ teaspoon salt

Soak the ground shrimp in the grapefruit and lime juices for 10 minutes, then mix with the rest of the ingredients. Serve at once.

Yield: Approx. 3 cups

SERVING SUGGESTIONS: This salsa makes a great addition to grilled fish such as tuna. Or, for a real treat, try it spooned over a baked potato.

PAPAYA SALSA

Papayas are available throughout the Southwest, and due to the Mexican influence in our cooking, southwestern cooks are using them more than ever. I find that the sweet, earthy flavor of the papaya teamed with the jalapeño makes me think of a trip to the beach.

2 medium-size ripe papayas, peeled, seeded, and diced

1 clove garlic, squeezed through a garlic press

½ medium-size red onion, finely diced

1 tablespoon chopped fresh cilantro

½ cup fresh lime juice

1 red jalapeño, membranes removed, finely diced (seeded optional)

Mix all the ingredients together and refrigerate for 1 hour before serving.

Yield: Approx. 2 cups

SERVING SUGGESTIONS: Try this salsa with a grilled fish such as black bass or with grilled shrimp.

PEQUÍN CHILE SAUCE

Rather than buy a prepared, bottled hot sauce, try making your own—it's better. But beware—a little of this very hot sauce goes a long way.

2 cups crushed pequin chile

1 large-size white onion, quartered

6 cloves garlic, coarsely chopped

2 teaspoons salt

1 teaspoon freshly ground black pepper

4 cups cider vinegar

Place all the ingredients together in a blender and blend until smooth. Strain and store in the refrigerator until ready to use.

Yield: Approx. 4 cups

SERVING SUGGESTIONS: A drop or two of this sauce is great in soups or stews. It's also great as a seasoning for dips or salad dressings.

GREEN CHILE SAUCE

The blend of green onions, garlic, very lean pork, tomatillos, and fresh green chile makes a sublime sauce that I feel is very southwestern.

1 tablespoon olive oil

1 medium-size white onion, diced

3–4 green onions, chopped with the green portion

4 cloves garlic, squeezed through a garlic press

½ pound very lean ground pork

6–8 tomatillos, chopped

2–3 medium-size New Mexico green chiles roasted, peeled, and diced

1 tablespoon chopped fresh cilantro

1½ cups water

½ cup white wine

½ teaspoon ground cumin

¼ teaspoon crushed oregano

1 teaspoon freshly ground black pepper

½ teaspoon salt

Heat the oil in a deep sauté pan and sauté the onion, green onions, garlic, and pork until the pork is browned through. Add the rest of the ingredients except pepper and salt and cook over medium-high heat until it comes to a boil. Stir in the pepper and salt, reduce the heat, and simmer uncovered for 10 minutes.

Yield: Approx. 4 cups

SERVING SUGGESTIONS: Use over eggs Benedict instead of hollandaise sauce, or with huevos rancheros. It's also outstanding spooned over hot white rice.

HOT PEPPER–ALMOND SAUCE

Hot sauces do not have to come in a bottle from the supermarket. I find it very satisfying to create my own. The introduction of almonds into a tomato-chile sauce gives it an opulent taste.

¼ cup slivered or chopped blanched almonds, toasted (see Note))

1 clove garlic

½ teaspoon crushed árbol chile

½ teaspoon salt

2 medium-size tomatoes, peeled and quartered

¼ cup red wine vinegar

2 tablespoons olive oil

Place the almonds, garlic, chile, and salt in a food processor fitted with a steel blade and chop. Add the tomato and vinegar and process. Add the oil and process again until smooth. Serve at once. If stored in the refrigerator, let come to room temperature before using.

Note: To toast the almonds, spread the nuts on an ungreased baking sheet, place in a 325-degree oven for 7 to 10 minutes or until the nuts are lightly browned.

Yield: Approx. 2 cups

SERVING SUGGESTIONS: This is a wonderful sauce to spoon over grilled meats. The blend of rich almonds with the árbol chile, smoothed into a fiery sauce with the tomato and vinegar, will add a richness to grilled chicken or baked white fish.

SWEET AND HOT PEPPER SAUCE

The slowly cooked peppers, tomatoes, onions, and chile make a delightful velvety sweet/hot sauce.

1 tablespoon olive oil

1 large-size yellow onion, chopped

3 cloves garlic, squeezed through a garlic press

2 large-size red bell peppers, seeds and membranes removed, diced

2 large-size green bell peppers, seeds and membranes removed, diced

6 medium-size ripe, red tomatoes, peeled and chopped

1 teaspoon freshly ground black pepper

½ teaspoon crushed árbol chile

½ cup dry white wine

Heat the oil in a heavy pan and sauté the onion, garlic, and bell peppers for 7 to 8 minutes. Stir in the tomatoes, pepper, chile, and wine. Cover and simmer over very low heat for 30 minutes or until the sauce is thick and clings to a spoon.

Yield: Approx. 4 cups

SERVING SUGGESTIONS: This is perfect with scrambled eggs or on a ham and artichoke frittata. It's also lovely ladled over a grilled fish such as halibut.

RED CHILE SAUCE

You can find red chile sauce served throughout the Southwest and used in many dishes as well as a marinade. Over the years I have experimented with many different versions of this versatile sauce and have found that the addition of both chicken broth and tomato sauce gives it a pleasing richness.

3 tablespoons olive oil (divided use)

1/2 yellow onion, chopped

2 tablespoons all-purpose flour

1 can (14 oz.) chicken broth

1 small can (8 oz.) tomato sauce

1 tablespoon white wine vinegar

3 tablespoons ground New Mexico red chile

2 teaspoons ground cumin

2 teaspoons salt

2 cloves garlic, minced

Heat 1 tablespoon of the oil and sauté the onions until limp. Heat the remaining 2 tablespoons of oil in a heavy frying pan, stir in the flour and lightly brown to make a roux. Then add the chicken broth and stir until smooth. Add the tomato sauce, vinegar, chile powder, cumin, salt, and garlic and cook over very low heat, stirring until smooth and well blended. Store any unused sauce in the refrigerator. This also freezes well.

Yield: Approx. 3 cups

SERVING SUGGESTIONS: You can use this sauce to prepare red enchiladas, serve with posole, or add to soups or stews. Also use it to marinate pork or brush it on chicken before broiling or grilling.

CUCUMBER, SERRANO, AND MINT SAUCE

The fresh, cool taste of the cucumber with the intense heat of the serrano and the touch of mint make this sauce the culinary equivalent of "fire and ice."

1 small serrano chile, seeded and diced

2 medium-size cucumbers, peeled, seeded, and diced

2–3 medium-size green onions, white portion only, diced

2 tablespoons chopped fresh mint leaves

1 cup fat-free plain yogurt

¼ teaspoon salt

½ teaspoon freshly ground black pepper

Mix all the ingredients together and refrigerate for 2 hours before serving.

Yield: Approx. 3 cups

SERVING SUGGESTIONS: Serve for dipping shrimp or crudités. Also great over grilled pompano.

TOMATO, ORANGE, AND PASILLA CHILE SAUCE

The earthy taste of the pasilla chile and the bright red-orange-yellow colors make this a festive, rich sauce for meat.

1 dried pasilla chile, stem removed

1 orange, unpeeled, seeded, and quartered

3 large red, ripe tomatoes, seeded, and quartered

½ teaspoon ground cumin

¼ teaspoon ground turmeric

¼ teaspoon salt

½ teaspoon freshly ground black pepper

Chop the chile in a food processor fitted with a steel blade. Add the orange (peel and all) and process until finely diced, then add the rest of the ingredients and process just enough to blend.

Yield: Approx. 2 cups

SERVING SUGGESTIONS: This sauce provides a great counterpart to baked fish such as cod. Or serve for breakfast with scrambled eggs and blue cornmeal muffins.

RED CHILE PESTO

Fresh red chile is a much-sought-after taste, but it is only available during the late summer and early fall. The flavor is rich and earthy and well worth waiting for.

3 fresh red Anaheim chiles, roasted, peeled, and seeded

3 small-size red bell peppers, seeds and membranes removed, quartered

1/2 cup pine nuts

1/4 cup olive oil

1 teaspoon salt

1/2 teaspoon ground white pepper

Place all ingredients in a food processor fitted with a steel blade and process until the mixture is finely chopped. Refrigerate until ready to serve. You can also freeze this, but it must be eaten immediately after it is thawed.

Yield: Approx. 2 cups

SERVING SUGGESTIONS: Place a little of the red chile pesto on a piece of dark bread and serve as an hors d'oeuvre, or serve with pasta for a once-a-year treat. Or freeze and enjoy all year round.

JALAPEÑO PESTO

This stellar mixture of cilantro, parsley, and jalapeños, accented with cumin seed and orange peel, is an extremely versatile pesto.

¹/₄ cup chopped cilantro leaves

¹/₃ cup chopped parsley leaves

2 tablespoons olive oil

3 jalapeños, stem, seeds, and membranes removed, quartered

2 teaspoons fresh lime juice

1 teaspoon grated orange peel

¹/₂ teaspoon cumin seeds

¹/₂ teaspoon salt

Place all the ingredients in a food processor fitted with a steel blade and blend until very finely chopped. Store covered in the refrigerator.

Yield: Approx. 1 cup

SERVING SUGGESTIONS: This is truly wonderful spread on crusty Italian bread or served with angel-hair pasta.

CILANTRO PESTO

I've found that there is no middle ground with cilantro. Either you love it or you hate it. If you love it, try this pesto with its blend of cilantro, parsley, grated Romano cheese, walnuts, and fresh lime juice.

1 cup chopped fresh cilantro leaves

½ cup chopped fresh parsley leaves

1 clove garlic

¼ cup freshly grated Romano cheese

3 tablespoons chopped walnuts

1 tablespoon fresh lime juice

¼ teaspoon salt

½ teaspoon freshly ground black pepper

2 tablespoons olive oil

Place all the ingredients in a food processor fitted with a steel blade and blend until mixture forms a paste. Store covered in the refrigerator until ready to use.

Yield: Approx. 2 cups

SERVING SUGGESTIONS: Great served with hot steamed vegetables such as zucchini. I also love this pesto on buttermilk rye bread and topped with some goat cheese.

# PICKLED CHILE

Pickling chile is an age-old custom in the Southwest. Before refrigeration and freezing, it was one of the safest and easiest ways to preserve chile.

I remember one year when this was served at every party we went to. It finally evolved into an informal contest with every host and hostess trying to outdo the next with the excellence of his or her pickled chile.

This was my entry—and, of course, the winner in my opinion!

3 green jalapeños, seeds and membranes removed, diced

3 red jalapeños, seeds and membranes removed, diced

3 yellow jalapeños, seeds and membranes removed, diced

3 green serrano chiles, seeded and diced

3 red serrano chiles, seeded and diced

6 Anaheim chiles, roasted, peeled, seeded, and diced

3 cloves garlic, cut into pieces

1 medium-size carrot, scrubbed clean and diced

1 teaspoon salt

1 tablespoon pickling spice

6 whole black peppercorns

1 quart cider vinegar

2 cups water

1 cup sugar

Place all the chiles, garlic, carrot, salt, pickling spice, and whole peppercorns in a large glass jar.

Bring the vinegar, water, and sugar to a boil and pour over the chiles. Let cool 2 hours, then seal and store in the refrigerator until ready to use. Let the chile pickle in the refrigerator for at least 3 days before using. This will keep in the refrigerator for two to three weeks.

Note: If you can't find all the different colors of chile, use whatever you can find.

Yield: Approx. 6 cups

SERVING SUGGESTIONS: This is a great side dish to serve with beef or cheese and crackers. I particularly like it served with blue cheese on baked crackers.

Because it is pickled, this dish is also great to carry to the beach or the mountains for a picnic.

# CHILE OIL

Not only does this oil taste great, but it also makes a decorative gift.

2–3 dried pequín chiles
1⅓ cups olive oil

Place the pequíns in a clean 350-ml. wine bottle that uses a cork. Fill the bottle with olive oil, cork, and let stand at room temperature at least a week before using. When the oil reaches the heat level you want, remove the chile and discard. Store the oil in the refrigerator and let come to room temperature before using.

Yield: Approx. 1⅓ cups

SERVING SUGGESTIONS: I use this versatile oil when making spaghetti sauces and when sautéing onions for a soup or stew. It will give a zing to any dish.

CHILE WINE

Try this sherry with chile for that extra touch of fire in your cooking. I often use this instead of prepared pepper sauces.

3–4 dried árbol chiles

3 cups dry sherry

Place the árbols into a clean 750-ml. wine bottle that uses a cork. Fill the bottle with the sherry, cork, and store at room temperature for at least a week before using.

When the wine achieves the flavor and/or heat factor you like, remove the chiles and discard, as the wine will continue to get hotter the longer the chile is left in it.

Yield: Approx. 3 cups

SERVING SUGGESTIONS: A small amount of this chile wine finishes off a soup or a chicken dish to perfection.

DEAD MAN'S VENGEANCE

This fiery vodka is great for making Bloody Marys, although a friend of ours declared after drinking one that perhaps we ought to call it "dead man's vengeance."

3–4 tepín chiles

3 cups vodka

Insert the tepíns into a clean 750-ml. liquor bottle that uses a cork. Fill with vodka, cork, and let stand at room temperature at least a week before using. Remove the chile from the vodka when it reaches the heat level you want.

Yield: Approx. 3 cups

SERVING SUGGESTIONS: Pour 1 1/2 ounces chile vodka over ice in a tall highball glass, add 1/2 ounce fresh lime juice, top with tomato juice, add a shake or two of celery salt, black pepper, and salt. Stick a rib of celery in the glass and serve at once.

LEMON-GARLIC-CHILE OIL

This piquant mixture of lemon, garlic, pequín chile, and olive oil will add life to any pasta dish. I also like to use it in salad dressings or vinaigrettes.

> *4 cloves garlic*
> *Peel of 1 medium-size lemon, cut into strips*
> *2–3 dried pequin chiles*
> *3 cups olive oil*

Alternately thread the garlic cloves and lemon peel on a bamboo skewer and place inside a clean 750-ml. wine bottle that uses a cork. Add the pequins to the bottle, fill with olive oil, cork, and let stand in the refrigerator for at least a week before using. When the oil reaches the heat level you want, remove and discard the chile, lemon peel, and garlic. Store in the refrigerator. Allow it to come to room temperature before using.

Yield: Approx. 3 cups

SERVING SUGGESTIONS: Pour in a cruet and serve with mixed cooked greens or salads.

CHILE VINEGAR

The zesty combination of pequín chile and garlic, along with the bay leaves and vinegar, gives a lift to any salad dressing.

4 pequin chiles
2 cloves garlic
2 bay leaves, broken in half
3 cups white distilled vinegar

Place the chile, garlic, and bay leaves in a clean 750-ml. wine bottle that uses a cork. Fill with vinegar, cork, and let stand at room temperature for at least a week before using. When the vinegar reaches the heat level you want, remove and discard the chile.

Yield: Approx. 3 cups

SERVING SUGGESTIONS: Use in place of your regular vinegar in salad dressing or to marinate pork, or use when pickling cucumbers.

CALIFORNIA GARDEN RELISH

We spent one summer in a small casita tucked away in a private garden in Los Angeles and reveled in creating all sorts of new-to-us goodies using the extraordinary fresh garden vegetables that are so abundant in California.

2 large red, ripe tomatoes, peeled and finely diced

1 medium-size zucchini, scrubbed clean, ends cut off, finely diced

2 medium-size avocados, peeled and finely diced

6–7 green onions, finely chopped with the green portion

1 red or green jalapeño, membranes removed and finely diced (seeded optional)

1/2 teaspoon salt

1 tablespoon chopped fresh cilantro

1 tablespoon fresh lemon juice

1 tablespoon olive oil

1/4 cup red wine vinegar

Mix all the ingredients together. Refrigerate for at least 1 hour before serving.

Yield: Approx. 3 cups

SERVING SUGGESTIONS: Serve with blue corn chips or bolillos (Mexican rolls). This is also great served with cold, thinly sliced roast beef to make finger sandwiches.

VEGETABLE
&
VEGETARIAN
DISHES

INTRODUCTION

I admit that I'm a little prejudiced, but I've never understood or had much empathy with anyone who does not like vegetables.

Even as a child I ate with relish and even gusto every vegetable dished up even though, if memory serves me correctly, they were as often as not limpid, slightly gray, and overcooked versions of their original selves. Even then I looked askance at other children at the table who played with their spinach and toyed with their green beans.

Today I still shudder when I hear friends tell me that they really don't like vegetables but eat them because the doctor or the media or I said they should.

Cooking southwestern vegetables or preparing vegetables southwestern style may make even devout vegetable haters into converts. I know that if you like zucchini, eggplant, and cauliflower you will enjoy experimenting with these recipes in which I add different types of chile to heighten the natural flavors of the vegetables.

 JALAPEÑO RICE

To paraphrase Gertrude Stein, rice is rice is rice—except when the rice is cooked in chicken stock. Then it takes on a wonderful, mellow, rich flavor without all the fat and guilt.

This rice dish goes one step further with the addition of sun-dried tomatoes and jalapeños and gives you a sense of warmth and well-being with every bite.

1 large-size yellow onion, peeled and chopped

5 cups chicken stock

2 cups uncooked extra-fancy, premium-grade medium-grain rice

1 teaspoon olive oil

6 sun-dried tomatoes, chopped

1 tablespoon chopped fresh parsley

1 jalapeño, seeds and membranes removed, finely diced

1/2 teaspoon salt

1/4 teaspoon ground white pepper

1/4 cup grated Romano cheese

Simmer the chopped onion in 1 cup of the chicken stock until soft. Stir in the rice and the rest of the chicken stock, cover, and simmer until the rice is tender and all the liquid has been absorbed.

Preheat oven to 350 degrees.

Coat an oven-proof baking dish with the oil and place the rice and onion in it. Mix in the tomatoes, parsley, jalapeño, salt, and pepper. Sprinkle the Romano cheese over the top and bake in a 350-degree oven for 30 minutes or until the mixture is hot through and the top is lightly browned.

Serves 4–6

SERVING SUGGESTIONS: Serve as a side dish with roast chicken and top this off with Mango Salsa (page 94) to perk up a midweek dinner.

SAUTÉED ZUCCHINI WITH TOMATOES AND ANAHEIM CHILE

A lot of wonderful vegetable dishes lose their visual appeal when spooned onto a serving plate. This mixture of lively zucchini, tomato, and Anaheim chile, however, has great eye appeal along with outstanding taste.

2 tablespoons olive oil

1 small-size white onion, sliced

1 clove garlic, minced

3 medium-size zucchini, ends cut off, scrubbed clean and sliced

1 large-size red bell pepper, seeds and membranes removed, chopped

2 medium-size tomatoes, peeled and chopped

4 Anaheim chiles, roasted, peeled, seeded, and chopped

1/2 teaspoon salt

1/2 teaspoon freshly ground black pepper

1 teaspoon crushed dried oregano

1 tablespoon chopped fresh parsley

1/4 cup crumbled feta cheese

Heat the oil in large sauté pan, add the onion, garlic, zucchini, and bell pepper and sauté for 4 to 5 minutes. Add the tomatoes, chile, salt, pepper, oregano, and parsley. Cover the pan and simmer for 6 to 7 minutes or until the zucchini is tender.

Serve topped with a small amount of feta cheese crumbled over each serving.

Serves 4–6

SERVING SUGGESTIONS: This is a smashing summer dish served with very thin slices of roast pork. To add an extra splash of color, spoon the zucchini, tomatoes, and chile mixture into a radicchio leaf.

SPICY BROWN RICE

My Aunt Naomi had definite opinions about food. She would preside over her long dining table with its spotless linen tablecloth and expound about the virtues of every dish she passed. I remember as a child assuming that rice was white, period—that is, until Aunt Naomi served brown rice and told us how good it was for us. It took me years to learn that brown rice not only is good for you but also tastes terrific when combined with chopped carrot, celery, pimento, and a fiery hot chile.

2 tablespoons olive oil

1 medium-size yellow onion, peeled and finely chopped

1 medium-size carrot, diced

3 stalks celery, back strings removed, diced

1 medium-size pimento, seeded and diced

1 cup uncooked brown rice

2 cups chicken broth

1 cup water

1 fresh Hungarian yellow wax chile, roasted, peeled, seeded, and diced

1 tablespoon chopped fresh parsley

1 tablespoon chopped fresh cilantro

1 teaspoon freshly ground black pepper

1/2 teaspoon salt

Heat the oil in a 2-quart Dutch oven or heavy pan with a tight-fitting lid, then add the onion, carrot, celery, and pimento. Stir and turn the heat down to medium. Cook for 10 minutes, then stir in the rice. Add the chicken broth, water, chile, parsley, cilantro, pepper, and salt. Cover and simmer over low heat for 45 minutes or until the rice is done.

Serves 4–6

SERVING SUGGESTIONS: This assertive dish is a perfect match for curried chicken or shrimp. Serve with a fruit ice to cool your mouth between bites.

BAKED CAULIFLOWER WITH TOMATO-CHILE SAUCE

Cauliflower comes alive in this dish. And, yes, you can use a low-fat Swiss cheese, but so far I haven't found one that tastes really great. So shoot the works, use regular Swiss cheese and enjoy the sophisticated richness of the cheese coupled with the earthy flavor of the cascabel chile.

1 medium-size head cauliflower

2 tablespoons olive oil

2 tablespoons all-purpose flour

1 cup tomato juice (preferably freshly squeezed)

1 tablespoon fresh lemon juice

1/2 cup grated Swiss cheese

2 teaspoons crushed dried cascabel chiles, with the seeds

1/2 teaspoon salt

1/2 teaspoon ground white pepper

Bread crumbs

Paprika

Remove the leaves and stalk from the head of cauliflower, separate into florets, and rinse in cold water. Put cauliflower in a large pot and cover with water. Bring to a boil and cook—or steam over water—until the florets are just tender. Drain and place in a well-oiled baking dish.

Heat the olive oil in a saucepan and lightly brown the flour to make a roux. Add the tomato juice and lemon juice and stir until smooth. Stir in the cheese, chile, salt, and pepper and cook over very low heat just until the cheese melts.

Preheat oven to 375 degrees. Pour the tomato-cheese mixture over the cauliflower, cover with the bread crumbs, and sprinkle the top with paprika. Bake in a 375-degree oven 15 to 20 minutes or until heated through and the top is lightly browned.

Serves 4–6

SERVING SUGGESTIONS: This is nice to serve in a more formal setting with lamb chops and fresh fruit.

BRUSSELS SPROUTS WITH YOGURT AND SERRANO CHILE

My Great Aunt Lettie was a fussy woman who kept the neatest kitchen I've ever seen and turned out some gorgeous meals. Brussels sprouts cooked in her own homemade tarragon vinegar and yogurt stands out in my mind because all the children, except yours truly, refused to eat them.

I have recreated this dish, and the addition of the serrano is mine. If serrano chile is too hot for your taste buds, substitute Anaheim.

1 pound fresh Brussels sprouts, with the outer leaves removed, washed; or
    1 (10 oz.) package frozen Brussels sprouts

2 teaspoons tarragon vinegar

2 cups fat-free plain yogurt

2 tablespoons chopped fresh chives

½ serrano chile, seeded and finely diced

½ teaspoon freshly ground black pepper

½ teaspoon salt

Cook the Brussels sprouts for 10 minutes in water to cover with 1 teaspoon of the tarragon vinegar added; or steam until the sprouts are just tender. If using frozen Brussels sprouts, cook according to package directions.

Drain the water off the Brussels sprouts, return them to the saucepan, and add the rest of the ingredients. Cook over very low heat until warmed through (do not let boil or the yogurt may curdle).

Serves 4

SERVING SUGGESTIONS: This is a different method of preparing this traditional Thanksgiving vegetable and goes well with roast turkey or chicken, or with rice and pasta dishes for a vegetarian meal.

FIERY VEGETARIAN LASAGNA

This is a richly layered, melodious combination of tomatoes, zucchini, greens, and olives laced with a fiery salsa.

1 (10 oz.) package lasagna noodles

2 tablespoons olive oil

1/2 medium-size yellow onion, finely chopped

1 clove garlic, finely minced

1 tablespoon finely chopped fresh parsley

1/2 tablespoon finely chopped fresh cilantro

1/2 teaspoon salt

1/2 teaspoon freshly ground black pepper

1 teaspoon crushed fresh basil leaves; or 1/4 teaspoon dried basil

1/2 teaspoon crushed fresh oregano leaves; or 1/4 teaspoon dried oregano

1 jalapeño, seeds and membranes removed, chopped

3 1/2 cups ripe, red tomatoes, peeled and chopped, with the juice (see Note)

1/4 cup Green Tomato Salsa (see page 98)

2 eggs

15 ounces low-fat ricotta cheese

1 cup cooked, diced greens such as turnip, mustard, or beet greens, drained

1 cup scrubbed, diced zucchini

1/4 cup sliced black olives

1/4 cup grated low-fat Swiss or mozzarella cheese

1/4 cup grated low-fat cheddar cheese

2 tablespoons fresh grated Romano cheese

Cook the lasagna noodles according to package directions.

Preheat oven to 350 degrees.

While the pasta is cooking, heat the oil in a frying pan and sauté the onion and garlic until they start to soften. Stir in the parsley, cilantro, salt, pepper, basil, and oregano. Add the jalapeño, tomatoes, and salsa in the blender, blend, then stir into the onion and garlic mixture.

Note: I don't seed the tomatoes. The fiber in the seeds is good for you.

Beat the eggs in a small bowl, then, with a fork, beat the ricotta cheese into the eggs a little at a time.

Drain the cooked lasagna noodles and lay them in the bottom of a lightly greased 9 x 13-inch baking pan. Make sure the noodles overlap. Spread half of the ricotta-egg mixture on the noodles, then layer half the greens, zucchini, olives, and Swiss and cheddar cheeses. Top with half of the tomato mixture. Repeat the process. Top with the Romano cheese and bake at 350 degrees for 45 minutes or until heated through and bubbly.

Serves 4–6

SERVING SUGGESTIONS: A slice of this lasagna coupled with a spinach salad, a little bruschetta, and a glass of dry red wine makes me want to sing the praises of Italian cooking Southwestern style.

STUFFED POTATOES SUTTON PLACE

Those of us privileged enough to know her prized an invitation to the Sutton Place apartment of Jeannette Fritsche, the well-known Manhattan-based public relations expert who headed up her own firm in the 1950s and '60s.

An ardent feminist with a great interest in nutrition before either became popular, Jeannette also was a great cook. This is an adaptation of one of her recipes that beats the restaurant version of a twice-baked potato hands down.

The pickling spices combined with the fresh New Mexico green chile give just the right touch of sweet and sour to these potatoes.

4 large-size white baking potatoes

¼ cup crumbled feta cheese

¼ cup nonfat or low-fat milk

¼ cup dry (French) vermouth

1 tablespoon finely chopped fresh parsley

½ teaspoon salt

2 tablespoons Pickled Chile (see page 120)

½ teaspoon ground New Mexico red chile

Preheat oven to 400 degrees.

Scrub the potatoes and bake for 45 minutes or until done. Remove the potatoes from the oven and cut each one lengthwise. Scoop out the pulp and mash with the rest of the ingredients, except the chile powder. Spoon the mixture back into the shells, sprinkle with the ground red chile, and bake at 400 degrees for 20 to 30 minutes or until potatoes are warmed through.

Serves 4

SERVING SUGGESTIONS: Splendid served with a grilled steak. This variation of stuffed potatoes is well suited to al fresco dining.

BROCCOLI WITH ONION, PARSLEY, AND PASILLA CHILE SAUCE

For years I was stuck in a rut, eating broccoli with melted butter or a little Parmesan and butter sautéed in a pan and spooned over the cooked vegetable. This sauce, made with wine and the pasilla chile with its raisinlike flavor, poured over steaming hot broccoli will make you forget you ever needed butter to eat this wonderful vegetable.

1 medium-size bunch of broccoli
1 tablespoon olive oil
4 green onions, chopped with the green portion
2 cloves garlic, minced
1/4 cup minced fresh parsley
1/4 cup fresh lemon juice
1 teaspoon crushed dried thyme
1 teaspoon salt
1/2 teaspoon freshly ground black pepper
1/2 pasilla chile, stem and seeds removed, crushed
1/2 cup white wine
1 teaspoon yellow prepared mustard

Wash the broccoli and cut off the tough part of the stems. Place in a large pot, cover with water, and bring to a boil. Reduce the heat and cook—or steam over hot water—until just tender. Place in a warm bowl and keep warm.

Heat the olive oil in a saucepan. Sauté the onions and garlic for 4 to 5 minutes. Stir in the parsley and turn off the heat. Let cool for a couple of minutes, then place in a food processor fitted with a steel blade. Add the lemon juice, thyme, salt, pepper, chile, wine, and mustard and blend.

Return to the saucepan and simmer over low heat until hot through. Pour over the hot broccoli and serve at once.

Serves 6

SERVING SUGGESTIONS: Great with a white fish such as halibut.

BROCCOFLOWER WITH ORANGE-JALAPEÑO SAUCE

I really like the hybrid combination of broccoli and cauliflower. Rather than slather it with butter, I prepare this simple citrus-jalapeño sauce with just a hint of nutmeg to pour over it.

1 medium-size head broccoflower

1/4 cup water

Juice and grated rind of 1 orange

1 jalapeño, seeds and membranes removed, finely chopped

1/2 clove garlic

2 tablespoons olive oil

1/4 cup plain or orange-flavored club soda

1/4 teaspoon nutmeg

1/2 teaspoon salt

1/2 teaspoon freshly ground black pepper

Remove the outer leaves and stems of the broccoflower and break into florets. Wash the florets, place in a microwave-safe bowl with 1/4 cup water, cover with plastic wrap, and cook on HIGH in a microwave for 5 to 6 minutes, or until the broccoflower is tender. Or steam over hot water on top of the stove for 10 to 12 minutes or until tender. Drain and place in a serving bowl.

While the broccoflower is cooking, place the orange juice and rind, jalapeño, and garlic in a food processor fitted with a steel blade and chop. Add the oil, club soda, nutmeg, salt, and pepper and blend until smooth.

When the broccoflower has finished cooking, heat the sauce in the microwave on HIGH for 1 minute, or in a saucepan over low heat for 4 to 5 minutes. Pour over the broccoflower florets and serve. Discard any leftover sauce, as it will not keep.

Serves 4–6

SERVING SUGGESTIONS: This method of preparing this hybrid vegetable gives it a real zip. It's impressive served with a grilled salmon or broiled chicken.

SOUTHWESTERN-STYLE FIELD CORN AND CHILE

The meld of very, very fresh corn, tomatoes, bell pepper, and chile sautéed in a black iron skillet makes your palate want to sing praises to this southwestern harvest.

My mother-in-law, Lyndell Morris, made this splendid dish every summer when the corn was ready. This recipe is exactly how she made it, although she always served it with a generous helping of stories about what her large family cooked and ate in her native Arkansas.

Although you can use white or yellow corn for this recipe, I think white is best.

6–8 ears of fresh corn (white, yellow, or mixed)

2 tablespoons olive oil

1 medium-size yellow onion, chopped

½ medium-size red bell pepper, seeds and membranes removed, chopped

1 medium-size firm, ripe tomato, chopped

2 New Mexico green chiles such as Big Jim or 6-4, roasted, peeled, seeded, and chopped

1 jalapeño, membranes removed, finely chopped (seeded optional)

½ teaspoon salt

½ teaspoon freshly ground black pepper

1 teaspoon chopped fresh cilantro

Using a sharp knife, cut the kernels of corn off the cob. Then scrape the cob to get all the juice.

Heat the oil in a large, deep frying pan (cast-iron works best) and stir in the onion and bell pepper. Add the corn, tomato, jalapeño, salt, pepper, and cilantro. Cover and simmer over very low heat, stirring often, for approximately 20 minutes or until the corn is tender.

Serves 4–6

SERVING SUGGESTIONS: This classic New Mexico dish is superb served for a Sunday lunch. Goes well with baked ham, lean roast pork, or baked chicken.

SANTA FE-STYLE MUSHROOMS

In one of my less lucid moments I bought and restored a 200-year-old adobe outside Santa Fe. Money ran short before we could buy kitchen appliances, so we decided that cooking on a wood stove and in fireplaces was authentic, romantic, and exciting.

But I soon found that this type of cooking occupied all my waking hours, so I became an expert at back-of-the-stove or one-dish meals. This remarkable combination of mushrooms, gold tequila (the tequila aged in casks that previously housed wine or liquor), fresh dill, and the bite of pequín chile was born.

3 tablespoons olive oil

1 pound mushrooms, washed and sliced

1 tablespoon chopped fresh parsley

2 teaspoons chopped fresh dillweed

½ teaspoon ground white pepper

½ teaspoon crushed pequin chile

¼ cup gold tequila

1 cup fat-free sour cream

Heat the oil in a deep frying pan or Dutch oven. Sauté the mushrooms for 5 to 6 minutes or until just tender. Add the parsley, dill, pepper, chile, and tequila and cook for 3 to 4 minutes. Stir in the sour cream and simmer over low heat just until warmed through. Do not overheat or the sour cream may curdle.

Serves 4–6

SERVING SUGGESTIONS: Serve over toast points or with rice or noodles. This is filling enough for a main dish; served with a green salad, it makes a great luncheon.

CHILE PASTA WITH SUN-DRIED TOMATOES

There is nothing more southwestern than sun-dried tomatoes. Surprisingly, I didn't discover the delights of these wonderful little gems that look like miniature red wheels until about 10 years ago. I've often wondered why it took me so long to discover them. They give sauces a rich, intense flavor that is superb with pasta.

I know that you're going to think I've taken leave of my senses suggesting that you put orange juice and club soda in a sauce for linguine, but believe me, if you don't want to load a sauce with butter or too much oil, this is a wonderfully rich alternative.

1 package (12 or 16 oz.) chile-flavored linguine

4–6 tablespoons olive oil

4 cloves garlic, squeezed through a garlic press

2 tablespoons chopped fresh basil

2 teaspoons chopped fresh oregano

6 sun-dried tomato slices, chopped or 2 tablespoons chopped sun-dried tomatoes

½ teaspoon salt

½ teaspoon freshly ground black pepper

1 tablespoon chopped fresh parsley

½ cup freshly squeezed, strained orange juice

¼ cup club soda

¼ cup freshly grated Romano cheese

GARNISH: *Sprigs of parsley, chopped black olives*

Cook the pasta according to package directions.

While the pasta is cooking, heat the oil in a large frying pan, stir in the garlic, basil, oregano, and sun-dried tomatoes, and sauté for 3 to 4 minutes.

Stir in the salt, pepper, parsley, orange juice, and club soda and cook over low heat for another 3 to 4 minutes or until the sauce is warmed through.

When the pasta is cooked, drain and place on a warm platter or serving plates, top with the sauce, sprinkle with the Romano cheese, garnish with sprigs of parsley and chopped black olives, and serve at once.

Serves 4–6

SERVING SUGGESTIONS: This makes a nice first course for an elegant southwestern dinner party. Serve with toasted bolillos and a salad of leaf lettuce and arugula.

MUSHROOMS, SPINACH, AND ANAHEIM CHILE BAKED IN PUFF PASTRY

This is a mouthwatering dish, piping hot out of the oven with the fresh taste of mushrooms, spinach, and the tang of the mild Anaheim chile.

1 9x15-inch sheet of puff pastry

Vegetable spray release

½ pound fresh spinach leaves, washed

¼ pound mushrooms, washed and sliced

¼ cup crumbled feta cheese

¼ cup chopped green chile such as Anaheim or New Mexico, roasted, peeled, and seeded

¼ teaspoon salt

¼ teaspoon freshly ground black pepper

3–4 fresh basil leaves, chopped

Raspberry vinegar

2 teaspoons olive oil

Spray a baking sheet with vegetable spray release. Lay the puff pastry on the sheet. If frozen let stand on the baking sheet at room temperature for about 10 minutes.

Preheat oven to 350 degrees.

Spread a layer of spinach leaves down the center of the pastry, then layer the mushrooms, cheese, chile, salt, pepper, and basil on top of the spinach. Sprinkle a little vinegar over the chile, top with another layer of spinach leaves, and sprinkle a little more vinegar on the spinach. Fold the pastry over the spinach on one side, then fold the other side of pastry onto the first and secure with toothpicks. Brush with oil and bake in a 350-degree oven for 20 minutes or until the pastry has puffed up and is a nice golden brown.

Serves 4

SERVING SUGGESTIONS: This is great served with a fresh fruit salad for a luncheon or a late-night supper.

NEW MEXICO CHILE RELLENO BAKE

Although I adore chile rellenos, deep-frying them in all that oil troubles me, so I like baking them in a casserole dish, where I can also use low-fat milk and egg substitute.

The richness of the steaming-hot custard-style casserole encasing the tender, flavorful chile is the ultimate in southwestern comfort food.

1 teaspoon olive oil

8–10 large, whole New Mexico green chiles, roasted, peeled, and seeded

8 ounces low-fat cheddar cheese, shredded

2 eggs or the equivalent egg substitute

2 cups nonfat or low-fat milk

1/2 cup all-purpose flour

1 teaspoon salt

1/2 teaspoon freshly ground black pepper

1/2 teaspoon ground cumin

1/2 teaspoon ground oregano

1/2 teaspoon ground allspice

Preheat oven to 350 degrees.

Coat the bottom and sides of a baking dish with the oil. Place the chiles, side by side, in the bottom of the dish. Sprinkle the cheese over the chiles.

Place the eggs in a food processor and beat. Add the milk, flour, salt, pepper, cumin, oregano, and allspice and blend until smooth. Pour the egg mixture over the cheese and chiles and bake in a 350-degree oven for 45 minutes or until the mixture has set and is lightly browned.

Serves 4–6

SERVING SUGGESTIONS: This makes an excellent focal point for a vegetarian brunch.

RICE CROQUETTES WITH ÁRBOL CHILE SAUCE

I love recipes for old-fashioned rice dishes such as pudding and croquettes. I bring these croquettes into the '90s with the addition of artichokes and the smooth, hot red chile sauce ladled over them.

FOR THE CROQUETTES:

2½ cups cooked white rice (prepare according to package directions, but use chicken broth instead of water and omit butter)

1 cup artichoke hearts, packed in water, drained and chopped

2 eggs, lightly beaten

1 cup finely crushed bread crumbs

¼ cup nonfat or low-fat milk

½ teaspoon ground cumin

¼ teaspoon ground allspice

1 teaspoon canola oil

FOR THE SAUCE:

2 tablespoons olive oil

2 tablespoons all-purpose flour

2 cups chicken stock

1 cup nonfat or low-fat milk

½ teaspoon ground árbol chile powder

Garnish: Sprigs of cilantro or parsley

Preheat oven to 350 degrees.

Mix the rice, artichoke hearts, eggs, bread crumbs, ¼ cup milk, cumin, and allspice together and form into croquettes the size of large golf balls. Place croquettes in a baking dish lightly coated with the canola oil and bake in a 350-degree oven for 20 minutes or until firm and lightly browned.

To make the sauce: While the croquettes are baking, heat the olive oil in a saucepan, stir in the flour and lightly brown to make a roux. Stir in the chicken stock, 1 cup milk, and chile powder and cook, stirring constantly, over low heat until smooth.

Pour sauce over the hot rice croquettes, garnish with cilantro or parsley, and serve at once.

Serves 4–6

SERVING SUGGESTIONS: This is an unusual and elegant side dish for a vegetarian meal.

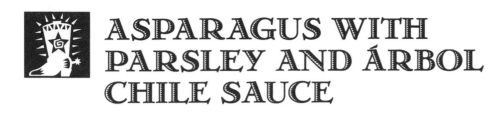

ASPARAGUS WITH PARSLEY AND ÁRBOL CHILE SAUCE

The bite of red chile paired with the fresh, just-picked garden taste of the parsley creates an appealing sauce for fresh asparagus spears.

1 bunch asparagus, washed

2 tablespoons olive oil

2 tablespoons all-purpose flour

1 cup chicken stock

1–1 1/2 cups nonfat or low-fat milk

1/4 cup chopped fresh parsley

1 teaspoon crushed árbol chile

1/2 teaspoon salt

1/2 teaspoon freshly ground black pepper

1/4 teaspoon turmeric

2 tablespoons dry (French) vermouth

GARNISH: *Sprigs of parsley*

Cut off the hard ends of the asparagus and place the stalks in a steamer over hot water or in a large frying pan with water to cover. Cover and steam for 6 to 7 minutes or until the asparagus is tender.

While the asparagus is cooking, heat the oil in a frying pan and whisk in the flour, then the chicken stock. Stir in the milk, parsley, chile, salt, pepper, turmeric, and vermouth and cook over low heat, stirring occasionally, until the sauce is smooth. Add more milk if the sauce becomes too thick.

Drain the asparagus and place on a serving plate or platter. Pour the sauce over the asparagus, garnish with sprigs of parsley, and serve at once.

Serves 4–6

SERVING SUGGESTIONS: Serve this for Sunday dinner with baked chicken or salmon. Also exciting as an appetizer.

RAVIOLI WITH ROSEMARY, YOGURT, AND PEQUÍN CHILE SAUCE

Now that fresh ravioli are so easy to buy in supermarkets, I usually forgo the dubious charm of making my own. Instead I create a memorable sauce to give the ravioli my imprint.

This intriguing blend of yogurt with fresh rosemary and red chile is a sublime sauce.

1 cup fat-free yogurt

1 tablespoon crushed fresh rosemary leaves

1 teaspoon crushed pequin chile

1 package (16 oz.) spinach ravioli (you can also use cheese ravioli)

1 ½ teaspoons salt

1 teaspoon ground white pepper

2 tablespoons chopped fresh chives

Freshly grated Romano cheese

Bring the yogurt, rosemary, and chile just barely to a boil in a large saucepan. Do not let boil or the yogurt may curdle. Reduce the heat and simmer over low heat for 10 minutes.

Cook the ravioli in water with 1 teaspoon of salt until done (7 to 10 minutes). Drain the ravioli and add to the yogurt-chile mixture. Add the remaining ½ teaspoon of salt and the pepper and gently stir to coat the ravioli with the mixture. Serve at once, garnished with chopped chives and freshly grated Romano cheese.

Serves 4

SERVING SUGGESTIONS: This makes a satisfying main course served with a green salad and hot French bread.

A MEDLEY OF SQUASH, MUSHROOM, LEEK, AND GUAJILLO CHILE

The crunch of the unpeeled squash along with the earthiness of the mushrooms and the guajillo chile, accented with the tang of the leeks, make this a perfect centerpiece of a vegetarian meal.

4 tablespoons olive oil (divided use)

2 cloves garlic, minced

3 leeks, well washed, white portion only, thinly sliced

2 ribs celery, diced with back strings removed

3 medium-size yellow crookneck squash, ends cut off, scrubbed clean and thinly sliced

1 pimento, seeds and membranes removed, diced

1 cup sliced button mushrooms

1 guajillo chile, stem removed, crushed with the seeds

2 tablespoons all-purpose flour

2 cups nonfat or low-fat milk

1 tablespoon chopped fresh parsley

½ cup grated nonfat or low-fat cheddar cheese

½ cup bread crumbs

2 tablespoons freshly grated Romano cheese

⅓ teaspoon New Mexico red chile powder

¼ cup sliced almonds (optional)

Heat 2 tablespoons of the oil in a large frying pan and sauté the garlic, leeks, celery, squash, and pimento for 5 minutes, stirring occasionally. Stir in the mushrooms and chile and cook for 3 to 4 more minutes, then spoon into a 9 x 13-inch baking dish.

Heat the remaining 2 tablespoons of oil and lightly brown the flour to make a roux. Stir in the milk and parsley (do not let the sauce thicken), and pour over the vegetables.

Preheat oven to 325 degrees.

Sprinkle the cheddar cheese and bread crumbs on top of the vegetables. Mix together the Romano cheese and the red chile powder and sprinkle over the bread crumbs. Top with sliced almonds, if desired, and bake in a 325-degree oven for 30 minutes or until hot and bubbly.

Serves 4–6

SERVING SUGGESTIONS: Serve as the focal point of a vegetarian dinner with fruit and crusty French bread, or as a side dish with turkey or ham for a special holiday meal.

SAUTÉED JÍCAMA, LEEKS, AND NEW MEXICO GREEN CHILE

This is a delicate blend of crunchy jícama, sharp leeks, and mild green chile that will remind you of the clean air and relaxed lifestyle of the Southwest.

2 tablespoons olive oil

3 leeks, well washed, white portion only, thinly sliced

1 clove garlic, minced

2 cups sliced, peeled jícama (sliced 1 inch long, ¼ inch thick)

2 New Mexico green chiles such as Big Jim or 6–4, roasted, peeled, seeded, and chopped

1 tablespoon chopped fresh cilantro

Heat the oil in a frying pan, stir in the leeks and garlic and sauté over medium heat for 3 to 4 minutes, stirring occasionally. Add the jícama, chile, and cilantro and cook for another 3 to 4 minutes. Serve at once.

Serves 4

SERVING SUGGESTIONS: This is a perfect side dish with broiled fish.

SPAGHETTINI WITH GARLIC, OLIVE OIL, AND POBLANO CHILE

This is one of my favorite vegetable dishes. I can walk into the kitchen after a late meeting or with only a few minutes notice to feed some unexpected guests, and the luxury of the oil, the bite of the garlic, and the mild heat of the poblano chile soothe my soul and satisfy even the most jaded palate.

16 ounces spaghettini

½ teaspoon coarse (kosher) salt

3 tablespoons olive oil

4 cloves garlic

1 large poblano chile, roasted, peeled, seeded, and diced

1 tablespoon chopped fresh parsley

1 tablespoon fresh lemon juice

Cook the pasta in boiling water with the salt for 7 minutes or until the spaghettini is *al dente*.

While the pasta is cooking, heat the oil and sauté the garlic for 2 to 3 minutes. Stir in the chile, parsley, and lemon juice and cook for 2 to 3 more minutes.

Drain the pasta. Using tongs, place pasta on serving plates. Spoon equal amounts of the garlic-chile sauce over each plate, and serve at once.

Serves 4–6

SERVING SUGGESTIONS: I like to make this my main course and top it off with fresh fruit such as a ripe pear and some great Jarlsberg cheese. It also makes a terrific first course, followed by a rich fish such as tuna poached in tomatoes and topped with olives and anchovies.

POBLANOS STUFFED WITH PASTA, OLIVES, AND ANCHOVIES

I loved stuffed bell peppers when I was a child. My maternal grandmother had a knack of finding all sorts of unusual things with which to stuff the peppers. My favorite was pasta and olives.

I've taken this one step further. I stuff poblanos not only with pasta and olives, but I add a decidedly Mediterranean touch: anchovies.

Orzo is a delicate pasta the size and shape of rice, often used in soups and broths. I like to use it for stuffings instead of rice.

1 cup uncooked orzo pasta

½ cup sliced black olives

3 anchovy fillets, washed and well dried, chopped

1 clove garlic, minced

1 tablespoon chopped fresh parsley

½ teaspoon freshly ground black pepper

1 tablespoon capers, drained

½ cup shredded nonfat or low-fat mozzarella cheese

6 large poblanos, roasted and peeled with the stems on, split lengthwise and seeded

1 teaspoon olive oil

Cook the orzo in boiling salted water for 4 to 5 minutes. Drain.

Preheat oven to 350 degrees.

Mix together the orzo, olives, anchovies, garlic, parsley, pepper, capers, and mozzarella. Divide mixture into six equal portions and spoon into each of the poblanos. Carefully fold one edge of the chile over the other and place the poblanos on a baking sheet that has been lightly coated with oil.

Bake in a 350-degree oven for 20 to 30 minutes. Serve immediately.

Serves 2–4

SERVING SUGGESTIONS: Serve this for a glamorous southwestern main dish with a jícama salad, cooked pinto beans, and warm flour tortillas.

SWEET POTATO, PECAN, AND ONION "PUDDING"

I think sweet potatoes are often overlooked in the search for vegetarian side dishes. I like the rich taste of the fresh sweet potatoes, accompanied by the crunch of pecans and apple, along with the depth furnished by the onions and cayenne.

4 large sweet potatoes, peeled and quartered

1 teaspoon coarse (kosher) salt

½ cup nonfat or low-fat milk

1 tablespoon olive oil

1 small-size white onion, chopped

1 green apple (such as Granny Smith), cored, peeled, and quartered

⅛ teaspoon ground cayenne

½ teaspoon salt

½ teaspoon freshly ground black pepper

2 egg yolks, beaten, or the equivalent egg substitute

1 cup chopped pecans

2 egg whites, beaten

Oil for greasing soufflé or baking dish

Cook the sweet potatoes in boiling water with the salt until the potatoes are tender. Drain and place in a food processor fitted with a steel blade. Add the milk and let stand until you've completed the next step.

Heat the oil and sauté the onion for 4 to 5 minutes or until soft. Add the onion to the processor along with the apple, cayenne, salt, pepper, and egg yolks. Blend until smooth.

Preheat oven to 350 degrees.

Stir in the pecans, then fold in the beaten egg whites. Spoon the mixture into a lightly oiled soufflé or baking dish and bake in a 350-degree oven for 30 to 45 minutes or until the casserole is set in the middle and lightly browned on top.

Serves 4–6

SERVING SUGGESTION: This is an unusual side dish for Thanksgiving in lieu of candied yams.

POBLANOS STUFFED WITH EGGPLANT

Although I love stuffed chiles, I try not to eat all the cheese and/or meat they are usually filled with.

This is a different twist. The earthy taste of the eggplant blended with the onions, tomatoes, basil, and the mild poblano chile is a tantalizing alternative to the conventional chile relleno.

1 small-size eggplant

1 tablespoon olive oil

1/2 white onion, diced

2 Roma tomatoes, peeled and diced

1 tablespoon chopped fresh basil

1/4 teaspoon salt

1/2 teaspoon freshly ground black pepper

1/4 teaspoon ground cumin

1/4 teaspoon ground allspice

1/2 cup bread crumbs

1 egg, lightly beaten, or the equivalent amount of egg substitute

4 large poblanos, with the stems on, roasted, peeled, and seeded, slit open lengthwise

Prick two or three holes in the skin of the eggplant with a fork, place in a microwave-safe dish and cook in microwave on HIGH for 6 to 7 minutes or until the eggplant has collapsed and its flesh is tender.

Alternatively, prick two or three holes in the skin of the eggplant with a fork, place on a baking sheet and bake in a 350-degree oven for 30 to 45 minutes or until tender.

Preheat oven to 375 degrees.

When the eggplant is cool enough to handle, peel and chop.

Heat the oil in a frying pan and sauté the onion for 3 to 4 minutes. Stir in the chopped tomatoes and basil and cook for 3 to 4 minutes more. Remove from the heat and stir in the cooked eggplant, salt, pepper, cumin, allspice, bread crumbs, and egg and mix well.

Spoon the mixture into the chiles, place in a baking pan and bake in a 375-degree oven for 20 minutes or until the dish is hot through.

Serves 4

SERVING SUGGESTIONS: This is a very rich dish. Serve with a simple lamb chop and have fresh fruit for dessert.

POULTRY
&
MEATS

SAUTÉED CHICKEN WITH WHITE WINE-PEQUÍN SAUCE

This dish is simple and easy to do. After coating the chicken in the flour and chile mixture and starting the sauté process, you can mix together the wine, lime juice, and chile that you will need to deglaze the pan.

This dish looks great coming to the table—with the lightly browned chicken, sparingly sauced, and garnished with green onions, cilantro, and lime slices.

You can omit the butter that finishes off the sauce; however, this small amount of extra fat smoothes and mellows it.

4 tablespoons all-purpose flour

2 teaspoons crushed pequín chile (divided use)

¼ teaspoon crushed dried tarragon

4 boneless, skinless chicken breast halves (3–4 oz. each)

¼ cup olive oil

2 cloves garlic, squeezed through a garlic press

½ cup white wine

2 tablespoons lime juice

½ teaspoon salt

1 tablespoon butter (optional)

GARNISH: *2–3 chopped green onions, sprigs of cilantro, lime slices*

Mix the flour, 1 teaspoon of crushed pequín chile, and the tarragon together in a shallow dish. Dredge the chicken breasts in the mixture. Heat the oil in a large frying pan, stir in the garlic, and then sauté the chicken breasts until done (approximately 10 to 15 minutes). While the chicken is cooking, mix together the white wine, lime juice, and salt. When the chicken breasts are done, remove to a warm plate or platter.

Pour the wine mixture into the pan and stir to deglaze the pan. Add the remaining 1 teaspoon of pequín chile and cook over high heat until the mixture is reduced and slightly thickened. Stir in the butter, cook for about a minute longer, and pour over the chicken breasts. Sprinkle the top with chopped green onion, garnish with the cilantro sprigs and lime slices.

Serves 4

SERVING SUGGESTIONS: I serve this marvelous chicken dish with confetti rice or a mixture of wild and white rice and arrange melon slices, strawberries, and green grapes on the plate.

CHICKEN BREASTS WITH RASPBERRY VINEGAR AND RED CHILE

Raspberry vinegar and chicken make a wonderful combination. Accented with a dried, crushed red chile such as an árbol or pequín, this dish takes on new heights. The yogurt-raspberry vinegar sauce is dramatically offset by the chile.

One preparation tip: I soak the chicken breasts for a few minutes in salted water to cover in order to improve the taste and texture.

2 tablespoons olive oil

4 boneless, skinless chicken breast halves (3–4 oz. each)

1 cup plain fat-free yogurt

¼ cup raspberry vinegar

1 teaspoon crushed árbol chile

½ teaspoon salt

½ teaspoon ground white pepper

⅓ cup sliced almonds

Heat the oil in a large nonstick frying pan and sauté the chicken breasts over medium heat for 10 minutes, turning once or twice.

Mix together the yogurt, raspberry vinegar, chile, salt, and pepper and pour over the chicken. Reduce the heat to simmer, cover, and cook for 10 more minutes or until the chicken is done.

Remove the chicken to warmed serving plates or a platter. Spoon the sauce over the chicken, sprinkle the almonds on top, and serve.

Serves 4

SERVING SUGGESTIONS: Serve with a medley of fresh vegetables such as zucchini, bell peppers, and eggplant.

CHICKEN BREASTS STUFFED WITH CHEESE AND PANCETTA

Chile, meat, and poultry stuffed with cheese are traditional southwestern dishes. Chicken breasts stuffed with cheese and pancetta (lean Italian bacon), accented with red chile powder and served with pan juices deglazed with wine and brandy, comprise an upscale southwestern dish that will delight your guests.

4 skinless, boneless chicken breast halves (3–4 oz. each)

Juice of 1 lime

1 cup all-purpose flour

1 tablespoon ground red chile such as New Mexico red

½ teaspoon salt

½ teaspoon freshly ground black pepper

4 strips pancetta

2 sticks string cheese (1 oz. each), cut in half crosswise

2 tablespoons olive oil

1 cup dry white wine

2 tablespoons brandy or cognac

Preheat oven to 325 degrees.

Place chicken breast halves between two pieces of waxed paper and pound until their thickness is reduced by half.

Rub the lime juice into the chicken breasts. Mix the flour, chile powder, salt, and pepper together and coat the chicken breasts with the mixture. Wrap each strip of pancetta around each piece of string cheese and then wrap the chicken around the cheese and pancetta. Secure with toothpicks.

Heat the oil in a large nonstick frying pan and sauté the chicken, turning occasionally, for 8 to 10 minutes or until lightly browned and cooked through. When the chicken is done, remove from pan and place on a warm platter or serving plates.

Deglaze the pan with the wine and brandy, stirring vigorously. Pour sauce over the chicken and serve.

Serves 4

SERVING SUGGESTIONS: Serve with Jalapeño Rice (page 129) or Chile Pasta with Sun-Dried Tomatoes (page 141).

GRILLED BREAST OF CHICKEN WITH LEMON-TARRAGON MARINADE

One of my favorite flavor combinations for chicken is tarragon and red chile. Together they produce a blockbuster chicken grilled over an outdoor barbecue or on a stovetop. The secret to the flavor in this recipe is to let the chicken marinate for at least 8 hours.

½ cup fresh lemon juice

1 teaspoon crushed dried tarragon

2 tablespoons olive oil

1 teaspoon grated lemon rind

½ teaspoon freshly ground black pepper

½ teaspoon crushed New Mexico red chile

6 boneless, skinless chicken breast halves (3–4 oz. each)

Combine all the ingredients except the chicken in a large glass container. Add the chicken breast to the marinade, cover, and refrigerate overnight. Turn the chicken at least once while marinating.

Remove the chicken from the marinade and grill about 6 minutes on each side or until done, basting at least twice with the marinade during the cooking process.

Serves 6

SERVING SUGGESTIONS: This is dynamite served with Spicy Brown Rice (page 131) or Stuffed Potatoes Sutton Place (page 136).

CHICKEN BREASTS ROSADO

Rosado means "rosy" or "rose colored" in Spanish and this dish lives up to its name. The delicate pink sauce served over the chicken breasts is underscored by the typically southwestern blend of red chile, cumin, and cilantro.

> *1 teaspoon olive oil*
>
> *4 boneless, skinless chicken breast halves (3–4 oz. each), soaked for a few minutes in salt water*
>
> *1 cup plain nonfat yogurt*
>
> *1/2 cup pink grapefruit juice*
>
> *1 teaspoon crushed red chile (arból or pequín)*
>
> *1 teaspoon ground cumin*
>
> *1 tablespoon chopped fresh cilantro*
>
> *1/2 teaspoon salt*
>
> *1/2 teaspoon ground white pepper*
>
> GARNISH: *1/3 cup sliced almonds*

Preheat oven to 350 degrees.

Lightly coat a baking pan with the oil. Place the chicken breasts in the pan and bake in a 350-degree oven for 20 minutes. Mix together the yogurt, grapefruit juice, chile, cumin, cilantro, salt, and pepper, pour over the chicken breasts, and cook for another 15 minutes or until the chicken is done. Remove from the pan to serving plates and garnish with the almonds.

Serves 4

SERVING SUGGESTIONS: Serve with rice mixed with small green peas, or ladle the lovely pink sauce over both the chicken and plain white rice cooked in chicken stock.

# CHICKEN WITH WHITE WINE, MUSTARD, AND PECANS

This is a unique blend of diverse flavors: wine, mustard, and pecans. You can omit the pecans to cut the fat content, but they make the dish so "*fino*" that I personally opt to cut out the fat in another meal instead.

4 boneless, skinless chicken breast halves (3–4 oz. each)

½ cup all-purpose flour

1 teaspoon ground New Mexico red chile powder

3 tablespoons olive oil

1 tablespoon chopped fresh parsley

2 garlic cloves, squeezed through a garlic press

½ cup dry white wine

1 tablespoon Dijon mustard

1 teaspoon–1 tablespoon crushed cascabel chile (amount depends on how hot you like your food)

½ cup chopped pecans

Juice of ½ lemon

GARNISH: *8 lemon slices, seeded; fresh parsley*

Place the chicken breast halves between two pieces of waxed paper and pound until their thickness is reduced by half.

Mix the flour and red chile powder together and dredge the chicken breasts in the flour mixture.

Heat the oil in a heavy frying pan and stir in the parsley and pressed garlic. Sauté the chicken breasts at high heat for 7 to 10 minutes, turning often until they are done. Remove to a warm platter placed in a warm oven.

Stir the white wine, mustard, chile, pecans, and lemon juice into the pan, deglaze, and heat until just hot, then pour sauce over the chicken. Garnish with the lemon slices and fresh parsley.

Serves 4

SERVING SUGGESTIONS: Serve with risotto and Sautéed Zucchini with Tomatoes and Anaheim Chile (page 130).

# RUTH GERBER TEICH'S TANGERINE CHICKEN

This is an adaptation of a recipe given to me by the romance novelist Ruth Gerber Teich. She calls for 6 to 8 dried pequín chiles in the recipe but recommends "if you're making this for the first time and want to start mild, either reduce the amount of pequins to 4 or serve with more white rice. By the way, don't eat those little red devils unless you have a cast-iron mouth."

Ms. Teich uses split boneless breasts or strips of chicken. When using the latter, she says, "I throw them into the pan with the sauce, cover for a while—20 minutes? I don't know for sure because I'm the kind of person who reads the wine label and dances on the ceiling."

As well as savoring the sweetly hot taste combination of the tangerine and the peppers, I also like this dish because it is so attractive, as the pequín chile used for cooking also makes a bold and colorful garnish along with the tangerine peel atop a bed of white rice.

2 tablespoons olive oil

¾ cup chopped white onion

Peel of 3 tangerines (divided use)

1 clove garlic, minced

4–8 dried pequín chiles, tops and stems removed, seeds remaining

2 cups fresh tangerine juice; or 1 can (16 oz.) frozen orange juice concentrate,
   undiluted

3 tablespoons dry white wine

4 boneless, skinless chicken breast halves (3–4 oz. each), or 1 pound skinless, boneless
   chicken strips

1 medium-size green bell pepper, seeds and membranes removed, diced

Heat the oil in an oven-proof pan and sauté the onion, the peel from two of the tangerines, garlic, and pequins in the oil for 4 to 5 minutes. Add the tangerine juice or undiluted orange juice concentrate and wine and simmer for 10 minutes. The sauce will thicken slightly.

Preheat the oven to 325 degrees. Add the chicken breasts or strips, cover, and bake in a 325-degree oven for 15 minutes. Remove the cover, add the bell pepper and bake for an additional 15 minutes.

Remove the chicken to a warm platter, spoon the sauce including the pequins over the chicken, and garnish with the remaining tangerine peel.

Serves 4

SERVING SUGGESTIONS: Serve this on a mound of white rice with a very cold "lite" beer.

ORANGE MARMALADE
AND JALAPEÑO CHICKEN

The blend of tart marmalade with the bite of both green and red jalapeño, accented with tequila and orange-flavored liqueur, gives this dish a great appearance and a deep rich flavor.

Try making your own marmalade for this dish. If you use a commercial variety, I would suggest buying imported Irish marmalade.

4 boneless, skinless chicken breast halves (3–4 oz. each)

½ cup orange marmalade

1 green jalapeño, seeds and membranes removed, finely chopped

1 red jalapeño, seeds and membranes removed, finely chopped

2 tablespoons fresh lime juice

1 cup fresh orange juice

½ teaspoon freshly ground black pepper

½ teaspoon ground cumin

1 tablespoon chopped fresh parsley; or 1 teaspoon crushed dried parsley

¼ cup tequila

2 tablespoons orange-flavored liqueur such as Triple Sec

Preheat oven to 350 degrees.

Wash and dry the chicken breasts and place in a roasting pan. Mix together the orange marmalade, jalapeños, lime and orange juices, pepper, cumin, and parsley and spread over the chicken breasts. Pour the tequila and Triple Sec around (not over) the chicken and bake in a 350-degree oven for 20 to 30 minutes, or until the chicken is done, basting occasionally with the pan juices. Remove the chicken from the pan and serve.

Serves 4

SERVING SUGGESTIONS: Serve with ratatouille or Wild Rice and Asparagus Salad with Chipotle Dressing (page 71).

A SOUTHWESTERN LIGHT CASSOULET

This is a lighter tasting version of cassoulet, which traditionally uses lamb and pork. The pasado chile gives this dish an appealing depth of flavor.

2 tablespoons olive oil

½ pound turkey sausage, crumbled

1 medium-size yellow onion, diced

1 medium-size green bell pepper, seeds and membranes removed, chopped

1½ pounds boneless, skinless chicken breasts, diced

2 cups chopped, peeled, cooked tomatoes

1 dried pasado chile, crushed

2 cups cooked white Great Northern beans

½ teaspoon salt

½ teaspoon ground white pepper

1 teaspoon Worcestershire sauce

Several dashes of Tabasco® sauce

Preheat oven to 325 degrees.

Heat the oil in a large, heavy frying pan and sauté the sausage, onion, and bell pepper for 3 to 4 minutes. Stir in the chicken and lightly brown.

Place the mixture in a baking or casserole dish. Stir in the tomatoes, chile, beans, salt, pepper, Worcestershire sauce, and Tabasco®. Bake in a 325-degree oven for 20 to 30 minutes or until the chicken is done and everything is hot and bubbly.

Serves 4

SERVING SUGGESTIONS: Serve with a green salad with fresh lemon juice squeezed over it and crusty French bread.

BROILED CHICKEN WITH TARRAGON-PASILLA MARINADE

Marinating chicken breasts and cooking over an outdoor grill with tarragon, which complements chicken so well, in combination with the pasilla chile gives this dish a distinctive flavor. One of the chiles used in making mole, pasilla imparts just a hint of the taste of mole to this recipe.

6 boneless, skinless chicken breasts (4–6 oz. each)

1 tablespoon crushed fresh tarragon leaves; or 1 teaspoon crushed dried tarragon

4 green onions, chopped with the green portion

1 cup dry (French) vermouth

2 cloves garlic, cut in half

1 pasilla chile, seeded and chopped

Place the chicken breasts in a shallow glass bowl. Mix together the rest of the ingredients, pour over the chicken, and marinate in the refrigerator for 1 hour.

Remove from the marinade and reserve the marinade. Broil the chicken over a hot barbecue or on a stovetop grill for 2 to 3 minutes on each side or until done, basting with the marinade and turning the chicken breasts two or three times.

Serves 4–6

SERVING SUGGESTIONS: Serve with Layered Cabbage, Potato, Pimento, and Arugula Salad with Fiery Vinaigrette (page 82) or Watermelon Salsa (page 102).

CHICKEN WITH ALMONDS AND POBLANO CHILE

This is a marvelous light mixture of chicken spiced with pequín and poblano chiles, accented with rosemary and almonds.

1 pound boneless, skinless chicken breasts, cubed into 1-inch pieces

½ cup all-purpose flour

1 teaspoon crushed pequín chile

2 tablespoons olive oil

2 cups chicken broth

½ teaspoon ground white pepper

1 poblano chile, roasted, peeled, seeded, and chopped

1 tablespoon crushed fresh rosemary

½ cup low-fat sour cream

¼ cup blanched slivered almonds

Place the cubed chicken in a plastic bag with the flour and crushed pequín and shake to coat the chicken pieces.

Heat the oil in a large sauté pan with a lid and sauté the chicken cubes, stirring occasionally, until they are lightly browned.

Add the chicken broth, pepper, poblano chile, and rosemary and cook covered for 20 minutes or until the chicken is tender.

Uncover, stir in the sour cream and almonds, and simmer just until the sour cream and almonds are hot. Do not let mixture boil or the sour cream may curdle.

Serves 4–6

SERVING SUGGESTIONS: Spoon into pastry shells or over cooked noodles or rice. Accompany with a green salad or a fruit salad with a light citrus dressing.

ROAST CHICKEN WITH RICE AND CHILE STUFFING

This is a great dish for a special meal such as an anniversary dinner for two. The rice stuffing with the mushrooms, celery, guajillo chile, and piñon nuts makes a savory, elegant dish.

This stuffing is also great as turkey stuffing for a southwestern Thanksgiving.

1½ tablespoons olive oil

1 small-size white onion

¼ pound fresh mushrooms, scrubbed

1 cup diced celery, back strings removed

1 dried guajillo chile, stem and seeds removed, crushed

¼ cup piñon nuts

1 tablespoon grated orange rind

1 tablespoon chopped fresh parsley

½ teaspoon ginger

¼ teaspoon freshly ground black pepper

1 tablespoon light soy sauce

2 cups cooked white rice

1 roasting chicken (3½–4 pounds)

GARNISH: *Strips of orange peel*

Preheat oven to 325 degrees.

Heat the oil and sauté the onion and the mushrooms in the oil for 5 minutes. Add the celery and chile and cook another 5 minutes over low heat. Stir the cooked vegetables, piñon nuts, orange rind, parsley, ginger, pepper, and soy sauce into the rice and stuff the chicken with the mixture. Roast for 1½ hours in a 325-degree oven or until chicken tests done, basting several times with the pan juices.

Loosely cover the chicken with a piece of foil and let stand for 10 minutes before slicing.

Serves 2–4

SERVING SUGGESTIONS: Scoop the stuffing out of the cavity onto serving plates. Slice the chicken and place beside the stuffing. Spoon a vegetable onto the plate—such as Brussels sprouts steamed with bay leaves and sage, or braised celery root. Garnish with long strips of orange peel twisted into an attractive shape.

BAKED CHICKEN COLORADO

This dish is not named after the state but after the wonderful, rich red-orange color and intense flavor that the red New Mexico chile gives the chicken while it cooks.

You can put together this simple dish in a hurry and let it bake while you entertain guests.

4 whole skinless chicken breasts (6–8 oz. each)

1 tablespoon coarse (kosher) salt

1 cup fine bread crumbs

2 teaspoons New Mexico red chile powder

½ teaspoon crushed oregano

½ teaspoon crushed dried basil

1 teaspoon lemon pepper

2 tablespoons olive oil

Preheat oven to 350 degrees.

Soak the chicken in cold water to cover with the coarse salt for a few minutes. Rinse the chicken under cold water and pat dry.

Put the bread crumbs, chile powder, oregano, basil, and lemon pepper in a plastic bag and mix well. Shake the chicken in the mixture, one piece at a time.

Pour the oil into a cast-iron frying pan or a baking dish. Place the chicken in the pan and bake uncovered at 350 degrees for 45 minutes or until the chicken is tender.

Serves 4

SERVING SUGGESTIONS: I particularly like this dish served with a potato soufflé or baked turnips and spinach, which you can bake in the oven at the same time as the chicken.

BREASTS OF CHICKEN WITH ADOBO SAUCE

Adobo sauce, a rich, red sauce made with chile, vinegar, tomatoes, garlic, and onion, is at its best used with poultry. Slathered on chicken breasts before roasting or grilling, it gives them a deep, intense southwestern flavor.

4 whole skinless chicken breasts (6–8 oz. each)

1 tablespoon coarse (kosher) salt

FOR THE ADOBO SAUCE:

6 ancho chiles, stems removed, coarsely chopped

3 dried guajillo chiles, pullas, or New Mexico red chiles, stems and seeds removed

¼ cup vinegar

½ cup water

½ cup dry white wine

1 large-size ripe tomato, coarsely chopped

2 garlic cloves, halved

½ teaspoon crushed dried oregano leaves

½ teaspoon freshly ground black pepper

2 tablespoons olive oil

1 medium-size white onion, chopped

2 bay leaves

Soak the chicken breasts in water to cover with the tablespoon of salt for 30 minutes. Rinse under running water and pat dry.

While the chicken is soaking, soak the chiles in the vinegar, water, and wine for 30 minutes. Then place the chiles and the soaking liquid in a blender. Add the tomatoes, garlic, oregano, and pepper and blend until smooth.

Heat the oil in a saucepan and sauté the onion until soft. Add the chile mixture and the bay leaves, cover, and cook over low heat for 1 hour. Discard bay leaves.

Coat the chicken breasts with the adobo sauce and grill over a barbecue for 10 to 12 minutes, or in the oven 20 to 25 minutes, basting once or twice with the adobo sauce, until the chicken is done.

Serves 4

SERVING SUGGESTIONS: Serve with corn grits or rice and a green salad with jícama.

BREASTS OF CHICKEN IN PIPIAN SAUCE

Pipian sauces, which were the precursors to moles, are made from pumpkin seeds. (See the following recipe for a turkey mole.)

The sauce for this particular dish is a rich, red sauce that clings to the chicken breasts and makes one think of Mayan princes and temples.

½ cup all-purpose flour

1 teaspoon New Mexico red chile powder

1 teaspoon freshly ground black pepper

4 boneless, skinless chicken breasts (4–6 oz. each)

3 tablespoons olive oil (divided use)

¼ cup water

1 medium-size yellow onion, chopped

3 cloves garlic, chopped

1 cup chicken stock

½ teaspoon ground cinnamon

½ teaspoon ground allspice

½ teaspoon salt

1 large ancho chile, stem removed, seeds remaining

*1 cup toasted pumpkin seeds (Note: To toast pumpkin seeds, spread the seeds on
an ungreased baking sheet and bake at 325 degrees for 10 minutes or until the
seeds are lightly toasted.)*

Mix the flour, red chile powder, and pepper together and dredge the chicken in the flour mixture. Heat 2 tablespoons of the oil in an oven-proof pan and sauté the chicken for 4 to 5 minutes, turning to brown. Remove the chicken and reserve.

Pour the water into the pan, add the onions and garlic and cook over medium heat for 4 to 5 minutes until the onions are soft. Spoon the onions, garlic, and pan juices into a blender, add the rest of the ingredients (including remaining tablespoon oil), and blend.

Preheat oven to 350 degrees.

Return the chicken breasts to the pan, pour the pipian sauce over the chicken, and bake in a 350-degree oven for 30 minutes or until the chicken is warmed through.

Serves 4

SERVING SUGGESTIONS: Serve with rice and Papaya Salsa (page 109).

TURKEY MOLE

Mole comes from the Aztec word *molli,* which means a combination or mixture. The origin of mole sauce is clouded in mystery and tall tales. Some historians have said that it is the oldest surviving recipe from the known ancient cultures or that this Mayan dish was first concocted by slaves of the Emperor Montezuma to be served to Cortéz.

Another story is that mole was developed several hundred years after the death of Christ, when an important visitor stopped by a poor nunnery in the heart of Mexico. The nuns did not have much to serve their illustrious guest, but they rummaged through their larder, threw everything they had into a large pot, and let it cook for hours over a wood fire. They then ladled this rich, dark sauce over an over-the-hill bird they'd caught and cooked. The dish delighted their company and soon became a requisite in the repertoires of Mexican chefs.

This is my version of this luxurious, slightly heavy sauce that clings to chicken or turkey and makes an almost sensuous statement at any dinner table.

1 skinless turkey breast (5–6-lbs.)

1 cup white wine

2 cups water

FOR THE MOLE SAUCE:

2 tablespoons olive oil

1 large-size yellow onion, coarsely chopped

3 cloves garlic, chopped

2 dried chipotle chiles, stems removed, coarsely chopped with the seeds

1 ancho chile, stem removed, coarsely chopped with the seeds

1 dried pasilla chile, stem removed, coarsely chopped with the seeds

2 large ripe, red tomatoes, peeled and chopped

3 tablespoons toasted sesame seeds

1/2 cup celery tops and leaves

1/3 cup sliced almonds

1/2 cup raw peanuts

1/4 cup raisins

1/2 teaspoon salt

1 teaspoon freshly ground black pepper

1/2 teaspoon ground allspice

1/2 teaspoon ground cloves

¼ teaspoon ground cinnamon

¼ teaspoon ground anise

1 ounce Mexican chocolate or semisweet chocolate

2 tablespoons balsamic vinegar

4 cups chicken stock

GARNISH: *Sliced almonds, sprigs of cilantro*

Preheat oven to 450 degrees.

Place turkey breast in roasting pan. Pour wine and water over turkey, cover with foil, and roast in a 450-degree oven for 30 minutes. Reduce the heat to 400 degrees and roast for 30 more minutes. Reduce the heat to 350 degrees and continue to cook for 1 more hour or until turkey breast is done.

While the turkey is cooking, prepare the mole sauce. Heat the oil in a large, heavy saucepan and sauté the onion, garlic, and all varieties of chile in the oil for 5 to 6 minutes or until onion has softened. Add tomatoes, remove from heat and stir. Let cool slightly.

Place the remaining ingredients except the chicken stock in a food processor fitted with a steel blade and process to finely chop all the ingredients. Then add the onion-tomato mixture and 2 cups of the chicken stock. Process until smooth.

Return the mixture to the saucepan. Pour the remaining chicken stock or the equivalent pan juices from cooking the turkey into the food processor and swirl around to get out all the remaining bits. Pour into the saucepan. Stir well, bring to a boil, cover, and simmer over very low heat for 1 hour.

When the turkey has finished cooking, remove from oven and let stand 10 minutes before slicing. Slice and pour or ladle the hot mole over the sliced turkey, sprinkle with a few sliced almonds, garnish with sprigs of cilantro, and serve at once.

Serves 6–8

SERVING SUGGESTIONS: Serve with sliced avocado or Mixed Green Salad with Piñon and Green Chile Dressing (page 88). Also great with rice or baked sweet potatoes.

TURKEY SCALOPPINE WITH CILANTRO AND RED CHILE VINEGAR

Sautéed turkey scaloppine dusted with flour and red chile and served with cilantro and a red chile vinegar brings a great southwestern touch to a Thanksgiving dinner.

1–1½ pounds uncooked turkey breast, cut into ½-inch-thick slices

½ teaspoon ground white pepper

1 cup all-purpose flour

1 teaspoon New Mexico red chile powder

¼ cup olive or canola oil

2–3 green onions, chopped with the green portion

1 clove garlic, squeezed through a garlic press

¼ cup Chile Vinegar (page 125)

2 tablespoons fresh lime juice

2 tablespoons chopped fresh cilantro

GARNISH: *Lime slices, sprigs of cilantro*

Place the turkey slices between sheets of wax paper and pound until they are approximately ¼ inch thick. Mix together the pepper, flour, and chile powder and dredge the turkey in the flour mixture.

Heat the oil and stir in the onion and garlic. Add the turkey and sauté for 4 to 5 minutes on each side or until done. Remove to a warm platter. Deglaze the pan with the Chile Vinegar and lime juice, stirring vigorously to loosen any of the particles that may have stuck to the pan.

Add the cilantro and cook over high heat for 2 to 3 minutes or until the mixture has thickened slightly. Pour over the turkey and garnish with lime slices and sprigs of cilantro.

Serves 4

SERVING SUGGESTIONS: This is best accompanied by a fresh cranberry-orange sauce, mashed turnips, and/or steamed Brussels sprouts. Also good served with angel hair pasta with a fresh tomato and basil sauce.

PORK SCALOPPINE WITH CILANTRO SALSA

Most supermarkets carry loin of pork that has been cut in scaloppine-thin slices. Use them as is, or if they are too thick, place them between two slices of wax paper and pound until they are approximately ⅛ inch thick.

I like to serve this dish to guests, as the thin scaloppine garnished with the lemon and parsley, alongside pasta or rice and topped with the cilantro, make both an extremely attractive as well as mouthwatering dish.

FOR THE CILANTRO SALSA:

1 cup chopped cilantro

½ poblano chile, roasted, peeled, and seeded

1 clove garlic

½ teaspoon ground ginger

2 tablespoons fresh lime juice

½ teaspoon salt

FOR THE PORK SCALOPPINE:

2 tablespoons olive oil

1½ teaspoons chopped fresh parsley

¼ teaspoon ground white pepper

½ poblano chile, roasted, peeled, seeded, and diced

4–8 pork scaloppine, ⅛ inch thick

GARNISH: *Thin lemon slices, sprigs of parsley*

To prepare the salsa: Put all its ingredients in a food processor fitted with a steel blade and process just until finely chopped. Do not overprocess.

To prepare the scaloppine: Heat the oil in a large frying pan. Add the parsley, pepper, and poblano and stir. Then add the pork and sauté for 1 to 2 minutes on each side or until just done. Do not overcook or they will become tough. Arrange on plates and garnish with lemon slices and parsley. Serve with the cilantro salsa on the side.

Serves 4

SERVING SUGGESTIONS: This dish is excellent with pasta primavera, rice, or sweet potatoes cooked in their jackets. The cilantro salsa also makes a good accompaniment to broiled fish.

JALAPEÑO-AND-GARLIC-STUDDED PORK ROAST

I love roast pork and have to resist the temptation to name every such recipe I write about "my favorite pork roast." This roast is so sublime, with the slow burn of the jalapeño offset with the orange juice and white wine, that it may just be my favorite.

1 pork loin roast (3–3½ lbs.)

4 jalapeños, seeds and membranes removed, quartered

6 medium cloves garlic

½ teaspoon salt

1 teaspoon coarsely ground black pepper

1 cup water

1 cup fresh orange juice

2 cups white wine (divided use)

Preheat oven to 450 degrees.

Wash and pat dry the roast. Place the jalapeños, garlic, salt, and pepper in a food processor and chop until blended.

Make several slits in the roast and, using an iced tea spoon or your hands, insert the jalapeño-garlic mixture into the slits.

Pour the water, orange juice, and 1 cup of the white wine into a baking pan. Set the roast in the liquid and place the pan in a 450-degree oven for 30 minutes. Reduce the heat to 350 degrees and cook, basting occasionally, for another 30 minutes or until the roast is done.

When done, remove the roast to a carving board and let sit for 10 minutes.

While the pork is resting, skim the fat off the remaining liquid in the baking pan, then place on top of the stove over high heat. Stir in the remaining cup of wine, deglaze the pan, and cook until the sauce reduces slightly.

Slice the pork and serve with the sauce on the side.

Serves 4–6

SERVING SUGGESTIONS: Serve with oven-roasted potatoes and a fruit salad.

MEDALLIONS OF PORK WITH TEPÍN-LACED PEAR SAUCE

The soft, sweet taste of pear with the bite of tepín chile, along with the rosemary and peach liqueur, give this pork roast an exciting, extremely satisfying taste.

8 pork loin medallions (3–4 oz. each), approx. ³⁄4 inch thick, well trimmed with all visible fat removed

1 cup dry white wine

1 tablespoon minced fresh rosemary

2 crushed dried tepín chiles

1 clove garlic, squeezed through a garlic press

2 tablespoons olive oil

1 teaspoon arrowroot

¹⁄4 cup water

¹⁄2 teaspoon salt

¹⁄2 teaspoon freshly ground black pepper

2 Bosc pears, peeled, seeded, and chopped

2 tablespoons peach liqueur

GARNISH: *Pear slices, sprigs of rosemary*

Place the medallions in a shallow glass bowl. Pour the wine over the pork, then sprinkle the rosemary, crushed tepíns, and garlic over the pork. Cover and refrigerate for 3 to 4 hours.

Remove the medallions from the marinade and reserve the marinade. Let the medallions stand at room temperature for 10 minutes.

Heat the oil in a large frying pan and sauté the medallions over medium heat, turning occasionally, for 10 to 12 minutes or until the medallions are cooked through. Remove the medallions to a warm platter.

Pour the marinade into the hot frying pan and deglaze the pan over high heat. Reduce the heat. Dissolve the arrowroot in the ¹⁄4 cup water and stir into the pan, then stir in the salt, pepper, pears, and peach liqueur and cook for 3 to 4 minutes.

Spoon the sauce over the pork medallions, garnish with pear slices and sprigs of rosemary, and serve at once.

Serves 4

SERVING SUGGESTIONS: Serve with sautéed zucchini or with a corn dish such as Southwestern-Style Field Corn and Chile (page 139).

PORK MEDALLIONS WITH SAGE, VERMOUTH, AND PASILLA SAUCE

This is a superb mélange of flavors and textures. The thin sautéed medallions in the sauce of dark, smoky pasilla chile and the herb-flavored dry vermouth make a fine centerpiece for dinner.

1/2 cup all-purpose flour

1 teaspoon crushed dried sage leaves

1/2 teaspoon cumin seed

1/2 teaspoon ground coriander

1/2 teaspoon freshly ground black pepper

1/2 teaspoon New Mexico red chile powder

8 pork loin medallions (3–4 oz. each), approx. 1/2 inch thick, well trimmed with all visible fat removed

3 tablespoons olive oil

1 cup dry (French) vermouth

1 dried pasilla chile, stem removed, finely chopped

GARNISH: *8 Roma tomatoes, stems removed, and quartered halfway through*

Mix the flour, sage, cumin seed, coriander, pepper, and red chile powder in a plastic bag. Add the medallions to the bag one at a time and shake until the pork is coated with the flour mixture.

Heat the oil in a large, nonstick frying pan and sauté the medallions over low heat, turning occasionally, for 15 minutes or until done. Remove the medallions to a warm platter.

Add the vermouth to the pan and stir rapidly over high heat to deglaze the pan. Reduce the heat, then stir in the pasilla chile and cook for 2 to 3 minutes or until the chile has softened and is warmed through.

Pour the sauce over the medallions, garnish with the Roma tomatoes, and serve.

Serves 4

SERVING SUGGESTIONS: Serve these with rice cooked in chicken stock and then mixed with warmed artichoke hearts, Greek olives, and sprinkled with safflowers (you can buy safflowers in Mexican markets throughout the Southwest).

HERB-ROASTED TENDERLOIN WITH RED PEPPER, PAPAYA, AND CHILE SAUCE

In my opinion the tenderloin is the juiciest, most succulent cut of beef. Topped with the bite of árbol chile integrated with balsamic vinegar, garlic, coriander, and the ripe, heady taste of papaya, you have a dish that will convince the most jaded palate that there is still reason to rejoice.

Note: I am adamant about not cooking meat with salt—not for health reasons but because adding salt to meat before cooking will make it tougher. My advice is to add any salt later, after the meat is almost cooked or fully cooked.

1 beef tenderloin (1½–2 lbs.) with all visible fat trimmed

2 teaspoons olive oil

1 clove garlic, squeezed through a garlic press

1 teaspoon crushed dried rosemary

½ teaspoon ground cumin

½ teaspoon freshly ground black pepper

¼ teaspoon ground oregano

FOR THE RED PEPPER, PAPAYA, AND CHILE SAUCE:

2 medium-size red bell peppers, seeds and membranes removed, quartered

1 dried árbol chile, crushed

2 teaspoons balsamic vinegar

1 clove garlic, quartered

½ teaspoon salt

½ teaspoon ground coriander seeds

1 papaya, peeled, seeded, and coarsely chopped (about 1 cup)

1 tablespoon fresh lime juice

GARNISH: *Sprigs of cilantro or parsley*

Let tenderloin stand at room temperature for 30 minutes. Rub the meat with a damp towel and then dry it.

Preheat oven to 400 degrees.

Mix together the oil, garlic, rosemary, cumin, pepper, and oregano and rub the mixture on all sides of the roast. Place the beef on a rack inside a roasting pan and roast in a 400-degree oven for 30 minutes or until done to taste.

Remove the beef from the oven and let stand for 10 minutes before slicing.

To make the sauce: Place the bell peppers, árbol chile, vinegar, garlic, salt, coriander, papaya, and lime juice in a food processor fitted with a steel blade and blend until well mixed.

Slice the beef and layer the slices, overlapping each other, on a platter, then spoon a line of the sauce down the center of the slices. Garnish with springs of cilantro or parsley and serve.

Serves 4–6

SERVING SUGGESTIONS: Serve with oven-roasted potatoes and a green salad. Also great with wild rice and a cold asparagus vinaigrette.

YELLOW SQUASH, NOPALES, AND ASADO BURRITOS

Burritos originated as a way for Mexican men to carry their lunch to work. Their wives would fill a flour tortilla, nicknamed a "burro," with meat, beans, and vegetables.

This dish elevates the lowly burrito to new heights. It is a delicate blend of *asado*—which in this case is round steak slowly cooked and then shredded—squash, and nopales.

The nopales are sliced from the large paddles of the nopal cactus, known as "prickly pear." They have the most wonderful, fresh, green taste. You can buy sliced nopales in most stores in the Southwest specializing in Mexican and Latin American food.

FOR THE ASADO FILLING:

1/2 cup all-purpose flour

1 teaspoon cayenne pepper

2–2¹/2 pounds boneless round steak, cut into large bite-size pieces

3 tablespoons olive oil

1 small yellow onion, coarsely chopped

4 medium ripe tomatoes, peeled and coarsely chopped

2 large Anaheim or New Mexico green chiles, roasted, peeled, seeded, and chopped

1 teaspoon New Mexico red chile powder

2 cloves garlic, minced

2¹/₂ cups water

¹/₂ teaspoon light soy sauce

1 tablespoon Worcestershire sauce

FOR THE BURRITOS:

2 tablespoons olive oil

1 medium-size white onion, sliced very finely, then the slices cut in half

2 medium-size carrots, shredded

1 cup nopales, cut into ¹/₂-inch strips

2 medium- to large-size yellow squash, sliced

12 large flour tortillas (9¹/₂ inches in diameter)

Asado filling (see above recipe)

2 large ripe tomatoes, chopped

GARNISH: *Sour cream and shredded cheddar cheese (optional)*

To make the asado: Preheat the oven to 350 degrees. Mix the flour and cayenne together and rub into the steak. Heat the oil in a heavy pot or Dutch oven and brown the steak. Add the onion, tomatoes, green chile, red chile powder, and garlic. Mix the water with the soy sauce and Worcestershire sauce and pour over the steak. Bake in a 350-degree oven for 2 hours or until the meat is tender enough to shred. Let cool enough to handle, then shred.

To make the burritos: Heat the oil in a heavy saucepan and sauté the onion, carrots, nopales, and squash for 5 to 6 minutes or until the squash is *al dente.*

If the asado is not warm, heat it for a few seconds in a microwave.

Heat the flour tortillas, 1 or 2 at a time, in a microwave on HIGH for 30 seconds or until warm. Do not overcook or they will become tough.

Lay the warm tortillas on plates and divide the squash mixture equally onto the tortillas, then top with a little of the shredded asado and some chopped tomato. Roll the tortilla around the mixture and top with a dollop of sour cream and a sprinkle of shredded cheddar cheese, if desired.

Serves 4–6

SERVING SUGGESTIONS: Serve with a pot of cooked Anasazi or pinto beans.

SOUTHWESTERN STIR-FRY WITH BABY CORN, JALAPEÑOS, AND NOPALES

Tired of stir-fry, you say. Have you had a stir-fry with cactus? Try this particularly southwestern dish featuring nopales—the edible paddles from the nopal cactus, which you just have to scrub off the thorns, slice, and eat—along with baby corn, which is eaten whole. Tossed together with a lean round steak, crisp jícama, and the sting of jalapeño, this is the *sine qua non* of stir-frys.

½ pound top round steak, all visible fat removed

2 tablespoons olive oil (divided use)

1 clove garlic, squeezed through a garlic press

3–4 green onions, chopped with the green portion

1 medium-size red bell pepper, seeds and membranes removed, sliced into ¼-inch strips

12–14 ears baby corn

1 cup washed and dried, thinly sliced nopales

1 cup peeled, sliced jícama, cut ¼ inch x 1–1½ inches long

1 jalapeño, stem and seeds removed, thinly sliced

½ teaspoon cumin seeds

½ teaspoon crushed dried oregano leaves

½ teaspoon freshly ground black pepper

½ teaspoon salt

Place the round steak in the refrigerator for at least 4 hours before slicing. Slice across the grain into strips ⅛ thick, cover with plastic wrap, and let stand for about 15 minutes before cooking.

Heat 1 tablespoon of the oil in a wok. When hot, stir in the beef and stir-fry for 2 to 3 minutes or until the beef is almost done. Remove the beef to a warm plate.

Add the remaining 1 tablespoon oil and stir in the garlic, onions, and bell pepper and stir-fry for 2 minutes. Add the corn, nopales, jícama, jalapeño, cumin seeds, oregano, pepper, and salt and continue to cook for 2 to 3 more minutes or until the onion and bell peppers have softened.

Return the beef to the wok and cook for 1 to 2 more minutes until the beef is warmed through.

Serves 4

SERVING SUGGESTIONS: Serve over rice with a green salad.

FOLDED SOFT TACOS AL CARBÓN WITH GINGER AND AVOCADO SALSA

The first tacos I remember eating were at a restaurant in Mexico and were made with grilled steak (*al carbón*). Although ground or chopped meat fills most tacos in the Southwest, I still prefer the wonderful sensation of warm steak cuddled in super-fresh flour tortilla.

Topped with red onion, tomatoes, cilantro, fresh green Anaheim chile, and a delicate ginger and avocado salsa, these tacos are surefire winners.

FOR THE GINGER AND AVOCADO SALSA:

2 avocados, peeled, seeded, and quartered

1 tablespoon lemon juice

1 tablespoon sweet pickled ginger with the juice (available in Japanese markets),
   or grated fresh ginger

1/2 teaspoon salt

FOR THE TACOS:

2 pounds rib eye steak, 1 1/2–2 inches thick, trimmed of all visible fat

1 teaspoon freshly ground black pepper

12 flour tortillas (8 inches in diameter)

1 medium-size red onion, sliced tissue thin

4 tomatoes, peeled, seeded, and chopped

1 tablespoon chopped fresh cilantro

6 Anaheim or New Mexico chiles such as Sandia or 6-4, roasted, peeled, seeded,
   and cut into strips

To make the salsa: Place the avocados, lemon juice, ginger, and salt in a food processor fitted with a steel blade and process until smooth. Refrigerate until ready to use.

Preheat oven to 350 degrees.

To make the tacos: Rub the pepper into the steaks and grill to the desired doneness. Let stand 5 minutes, then thinly slice across the grain.

Wet a clean tea towel and lay half of it in a shallow baking pan large enough to hold the tortillas. Place the tortillas on the towel, fold it over to cover them, and heat in a 350 degree oven for 15 minutes or until the tortillas have steamed through and are warm. Alternatively, you can heat the tortillas, one at a time, in a microwave on HIGH for 15 to 30 seconds or just until they are warm.

Divide the steak into 12 equal portions and place each portion on one half of each tortilla. Top with some of the red onion, tomato, cilantro, and 1 or 2 green chile strips. Drizzle approximately 1 tablespoon of the avocado salsa over the chile strips, fold the tortillas over, and serve.

Serves 6

SERVING SUGGESTIONS: Serve with a bowl of pinto beans, Spanish rice, or a green salad.

LAMB CHOPS BAKED IN CHILE AND BEER

The subtle flavor of the poblano chile, in tandem with the beer and accented by garlic and onion, produces lamb chops that are truly unforgettable.

A plus is that you can come home from work, assemble this dish, and have dinner on the table in 45 minutes.

2 tablespoons olive oil

1/2 medium-size yellow onion, peeled and diced

2 cloves garlic, peeled and chopped

1 medium-size green bell pepper, seeds and membranes removed, diced

8 lamb chops (3–4 oz. each)

1 poblano chile, roasted, peeled, seeded, and stem removed, diced

2 bay leaves

1/2 teaspoon freshly ground black pepper

2 cans (12 oz. each) "lite" beer

Preheat oven to 350 degrees.

Heat the oil in a heavy Dutch oven and sauté the onion, garlic, and bell pepper until onion is softened. Add the chops and brown on both sides. Add the rest of the ingredients and bake in a 350-degree oven for 20 to 30 minutes or until done to your taste. Remove the bay leaves and serve.

Serves 4

SERVING SUGGESTIONS: Serve with oven-roasted new potatoes, pasta, or rice.

GRILLED ROSEMARY LAMB CHOPS WITH ROASTED GREEN AND YELLOW CHILES

This is an impressive dish, with the lean lamb chops marinated in fresh rosemary and pequín chile, grilled to perfection, then arranged on your best dinnerware and topped with vibrant green and yellow roasted chiles.

A tip to remember: In order to keep meat from becoming tough while cooking, after marinating or storing any meat in the refrigerator do not cook it immediately after you take it out. Let it stand at room temperature before putting on the flame or heat.

8 lamb chops (3–4 oz. each)

2 tablespoons chopped fresh rosemary

1/2 cup olive oil (divided use)

Juice of 2 limes

1 teaspoon crushed pequín chile

6 large New Mexico chiles such as Big Jims or Sandias

3 yellow wax chiles

Arrange the chops in a shallow dish. Mix the rosemary, 1/4 cup olive oil, lime juice, and pequín chile and pour over the chops. Cover and marinate in the refrigerator for 3 to 4 hours. Remove and let stand at room temperature for 1/2 hour before cooking.

Brush the chile with the remaining 1/4 cup olive oil and roast over a hot grill. When the skin has blistered, remove from the grill and, using rubber gloves, peel, slice into strips, and place on a warm plate. Grill the chops until done to taste, then arrange the peppers over the meat.

Serves 4

SERVING SUGGESTIONS: Serve with risotto and Mango Salsa (page 94).

ROAST RACK OF LAMB WITH ORANGE-PEQUÍN SAUCE

Moist, rare rack of lamb laced with orange, honey, and the nip of crushed pequín chile is the perfect main course to build a meal around when entertaining or for a Passover or Easter dinner.

1 rack of lamb (approx. 4½–5 lbs.)

1 tablespoon crushed fresh rosemary

1 teaspoon coarsely ground black pepper

½ cup fresh orange juice

1 ounce orange liqueur

1 cup water

2 tablespoons orange blossom honey

1 teaspoon salt

1 teaspoon grated orange peel

1 teaspoon crushed pequín chile

¼ cup dry white wine

Preheat oven to 375 degrees.

Place the lamb in a roasting pan and rub the rosemary and pepper into it. Mix the orange juice, orange liqueur, water, honey, salt, orange peel, and pequín together and pour over the lamb. Roast in a 375-degree oven, basting occasionally, for 45 minutes or until the lamb is done to taste.

Remove from the oven and let stand for 10 minutes before carving.

While the roast is resting, place the roasting pan on top of the stove and skim off the fat. Turn the heat up, pour in the wine and deglaze the pan, stirring hard to loosen any bits of meat. Stir until you have a smooth sauce. Serve on the side with the sliced lamb.

Serves 4–6

SERVING SUGGESTIONS: Start the meal with Hearts of Palm with Cucumber-Chipotle Dressing (page 76) and serve the lamb with baked potatoes topped with a healthy dollop of Pickled Ginger Salsa (page 105). Follow the meal with a cooling fruit ice for dessert.

FISH
&
SEAFOOD

RED SNAPPER WITH JALAPEÑO AND NEW MEXICO RED CHILE

This is a southwestern version of red snapper Veracruz. The blend of red snapper with tomatoes, onion, and garlic highlighted by the bite of jalapeño and New Mexico red chile powder makes your taste buds sing.

Tip: I find that microwaving fish such as this red snapper is the easiest, quickest way to prepare it. If you're one of those holdouts without a microwave, you can bake this in a conventional oven at 350 degrees for 15 to 20 minutes or until the fish is done.

4 red snapper fillets (about 1 lb. total)

3 medium-size red, ripe tomatoes, chopped

1 clove garlic, chopped

1 jalapeño, seeded and chopped

½ medium-size red onion, thinly sliced

½ teaspoon New Mexico red chile powder

¼ teaspoon crushed dried oregano

¼ teaspoon ground cumin

1 tablespoon fresh lemon juice

Grated Romano cheese (optional)

GARNISH: *Lemon wedges, sprigs of parsley*

Arrange the fish fillets in a microwave-safe dish, and cover with plastic wrap. Mix together the rest of the ingredients and pour over the fish. Microwave on HIGH for 3 to 4 minutes. Turn the dish, then cook on HIGH for 4 to 5 more minutes or until the fish flakes easily when tested with a fork.

Top the fish with a little grated Romano cheese, if you wish, and garnish with lemon wedges and sprigs of parsley.

Serves 4

SERVING SUGGESTIONS: Serve with rice and a salad of endive and curly lettuce.

RED SNAPPER-SERRANO CAKES WITH ASPARAGUS SAUCE

This is my variation of the classic crab or salmon cakes. The delicate flesh of the red snapper is highlighted by the sharp, peppery bite of serrano chile, offset by the crunch of pecans and a touch of orange and mellowed out with southwestern corn grits.

I sauce this with a smooth, velvety blend of asparagus highlighted with just a hint of cayenne. Since asparagus grows wild in many areas of the Southwest, many of us collect or buy it to freeze for later use. If left too long in the freezer, the asparagus may become mushy, and that is how this recipe was born. In an attempt to use asparagus that had been tucked in the back of our freezer and was no longer crisp, I devised this sauce. It's a wonderful finishing touch to broiled fish or seafood cakes or loaves. It is also tasty over simple broiled chicken.

FOR THE RED SNAPPER CAKES:

1/2 pound cooked red snapper, coarsely chopped

1 serrano chile, stemmed, seeded, and chopped

1 tablespoon chopped fresh cilantro

1 teaspoon grated orange rind

1/2 cup finely chopped pecans

1 tablespoon chopped fresh parsley

1 egg, beaten

1/4 cup bread crumbs

1/4 cup yellow corn grits

1 tablespoon fresh lime juice

1/4 cup plain fat-free yogurt

Dash of salt

Dash of freshly ground black pepper

3 tablespoons olive oil

FOR THE ASPARAGUS SAUCE:

6–8 stalks cooked asparagus, each stalk cut into 3 or 4 pieces

3 cups chicken stock or broth (divided use)

2 tablespoons olive oil

2 tablespoons all-purpose flour

1 cup nonfat or low-fat milk

1/8 teaspoon cayenne pepper

GARNISH: 4 green onions, slit in two lengthwise

To make the cakes: Combine the red snapper, serrano chile, cilantro, orange rind, pecans, parsley, egg, bread crumbs, corn grits, lime juice, yogurt, salt, and pepper in a bowl and mix well. Then form the mixture into 8 cakes each about 1/2 inch thick.

Heat the oil in a nonstick frying pan and sauté 4 cakes at a time until browned on both sides. Remove to a warm platter and drain on paper towels.

To make the sauce: Place the asparagus and 1 cup of the chicken stock in a blender fitted with a steel blade and puree.

Heat the oil in a frying pan, stir in the flour to make a roux, stirring until lightly browned. Stir in the remaining chicken stock, milk, and cayenne and cook, stirring, until smooth. Stir in the asparagus puree and cook, stirring constantly. If the sauce is too thick, add a little more milk. Spoon a little of the asparagus sauce over the red snapper-serrano cakes, and garnish with a green onion, slit in two lengthwise.

Serves 4

SERVING SUGGESTIONS: This is a nice dish to serve with a pasta salad.

SALMON STEAKS WITH A CHIPOTLE-MUSTARD MARINADE

The smoky quality of the chipotle chile deftly orchestrated with stone-ground mustard, green onion, capers, and yogurt creates a superlative marinade for broiling salmon steaks.

4 salmon steaks, 1 inch thick (approx. 6 oz. each), skinned and boned

¼ cup plain fat-free yogurt

¼ cup dry white wine

2 teaspoons capers, drained

1 tablespoon stone-ground mustard

½ teaspoon crushed chipotle chile

1 green onion, both white and green portions

Arrange the salmon steaks on a broiler pan. Put the remaining ingredients in a food processor fitted with a steel blade and blend until smooth.

Spread the mixture on the salmon steaks and broil about 4 inches from the heat for approximately 6 minutes on each side or until done.

Serves 4

SERVING SUGGESTIONS: This is terrific served with a wilted or steamed green such as spinach.

SALMON POACHED IN RED PEPPER SAUCE WITH SNOW PEAS AND SLICED CORN

This dish, with the delicate pink salmon offset with bright red bell pepper and fresh red Anaheim or New Mexico chiles, green snow peas, and slices of corn, is as attractive visually as it is tasty.

The use of sliced corn-on-the-cob is common in Latin and South America. I use it in many southwestern dishes combined with poultry, fish, or vegetables.

Although fresh red chile is available only in the late summer or early fall, it is worth waiting for to put that unique, special taste into this dish.

2 large red bell peppers, seeds and membranes removed, quartered

4 large mild, fresh (not dried) red Anaheim or New Mexico chiles such as Big Jim or 6-4, roasted, stems and seeds removed

1 tablespoon chopped fresh cilantro

¼ teaspoon salt

¼ teaspoon freshly ground black pepper

2 cups water

4 salmon fillets (approx. 4 oz. each)

2 cups snow peas or snap peas, stringed

2 ears of corn (fresh or frozen), sliced into 1- or 2-inch rounds

Place the bell peppers in a food processor fitted with a steel blade and chop. Add the chiles, cilantro, salt, pepper, and water and blend until smooth.

Pour the mixture into a large, deep frying or sauté pan and bring to a boil. Reduce the heat to simmer and add the salmon. Poach the salmon over very low heat for 8 to 10 minutes or until the fish flakes easily when tested with a fork.

While the fish is cooking, bring a saucepan of water to a boil, add the peas and corn, and cook or steam for 4 to 5 minutes. Drain and place equal portions on one side of each of 4 serving plates.

When the fish is done, carefully remove from the poaching liquid and place on the plates with the vegetables.

Turn the heat up on the chile mixture that the fish was poached in and boil for 2 minutes or until the mixture reduces slightly. Spoon over the fish and serve at once.

Serves 4

SERVING SUGGESTIONS: This is good served with risotto.

BAKED HALIBUT STEAKS WITH JALAPEÑO-GRAPEFRUIT VINAIGRETTE

Fish and citrus just seem to be natural companions. Most people think of lemon or lime with fish, but I like to add grapefruit juice with lemon and chile for a truly southwestern, tangy fish dish.

FOR THE VINAIGRETTE:

1 lemon, ends cut off, seeded and quartered

1/2 cup pink grapefruit juice

1 tablespoon olive oil

3 green onions, white portion only, sliced

1 jalapeño, seeds and membranes removed, quartered

1 tablespoon chopped cilantro

1/4 teaspoon salt

1/4 teaspoon freshly ground black pepper

FOR THE HALIBUT:

4 halibut steaks (approx. 5–6 oz. each), 1/2 inch thick

1/4 cup dry white wine

1/2 cup chicken broth

4 green onions, white portion only, sliced

1 tablespoon crushed fresh thyme; or 1 teaspoon crushed dried thyme

1/4 teaspoon freshly ground black pepper

1/2 teaspoon ground New Mexico red chile powder

To prepare the vinaigrette: Place the lemon in a food processor fitted with a steel blade and chop. Add the rest of the ingredients and blend.

Preheat oven to 400 degrees. Place the halibut steaks in a baking dish and pour the wine and chicken broth over the fish. Top with the sliced onions and thyme. Sprinkle with black pepper and chile powder and bake in a 400-degree oven, uncovered, 10 to 12 minutes or until the fish flakes easily when tested with a fork. Carefully lift the fish out of the pan and onto serving plates. Serve with the jalapeño-grapefruit vinaigrette.

SERVING SUGGESTIONS: Makes a nice meal with mixed brown, white, or wild rice or a warm pasta salad. You can also serve the jalapeño-grapefruit vinaigrette with broiled chicken.

BAKED HADDOCK WITH PEQUÍN CHILE AND CAPERS

This dish might not have started life being strictly southwestern, but I love it and so have unofficially adopted it as nouvelle southwestern fare.

The tart, slightly vinegary taste of the capers with one of my favorite chiles, pequín, gives the baked haddock fillets a taste that reminds me of sitting on the deck of a superb restaurant on the coast of Spain.

For this recipe I like to use a blush wine such as white Zinfandel.

4 haddock fillets (approx. 4–6 oz. each)

½ teaspoon freshly ground black pepper

2 tablespoons fresh lemon juice

1 red onion, thinly sliced

1 clove garlic, minced

3 large red, ripe tomatoes, peeled, seeded, and chopped

1 tablespoon chopped fresh parsley

½ teaspoon crushed pequin chile

2 tablespoons capers, drained

½ cup blush wine

½ cup water

Preheat oven to 375 degrees.

Rub the fillets with pepper and lemon juice and place in a shallow glass baking dish.

Lay the sliced onion over the fish. Sprinkle the garlic, chopped tomatoes, parsley, pequín, and capers over the onion. Mix together the wine and water and gently pour around the fish.

Cover and bake in a 375-degree oven for 15 minutes. Uncover, baste with the pan juices, and bake for another 5 to 10 minutes or until the fish is cooked through and flakes easily when tested with a fork. Carefully lift the fish out of the pan juices. Spoon some of the onion, tomato, and juice over the fish before serving

Serves 4

SERVING SUGGESTIONS: Serve on a bed of mixed greens for a festive look.

SCROD WITH GUAJILLO CHILE AND TOMATOES

The bite of green chile pasta together with scrod, tomatoes, and guajillo chile makes a positively sybaritic dish. Scrod, a small cod with a delicate, mild, sweet, firm white flesh, is readily available in southwestern markets.

12 ounces green chile pasta or fusilli

1 lemon

1 clove garlic, chopped

1 guajillo chile, stem and seeds removed

4 large tomatoes, peeled and quartered

1 tablespoon chopped fresh parsley

½ teaspoon crushed dried oregano

½ cup white wine

1 pound scrod, cut into strips 2 inches wide

Cook the pasta in salted water according to package directions. Make the following sauce while the pasta is cooking.

Cut the ends off the lemon, quarter, seed, and chop it in a food processor fitted with a steel blade. Add the garlic and the chile and chop until fine. Add the tomatoes, parsley, and oregano and pulse 3 to 4 times to blend.

Spoon the mixture into a large, deep frying pan. Rinse out the processor with the wine and pour wine into the pan. Cook until this mixture bubbles, then add the fish. Turn down the heat to low, cover, and simmer for 4 to 5 minutes or until the fish is tender. Spoon the mixture over the hot, drained pasta and serve at once.

Serves 4

SERVING SUGGESTIONS: Serve with chilled semisweet white wine and sesame breadsticks.

SOUTHWESTERN-STYLE OVEN-POACHED FISH

Our Southwest is more than just a region—it is a style of living. One of the things that makes living in the Southwest incomparable is that we take the best from the rest of the country and the rest of the world and give it our indelible southwestern stamp or style.

That's what I've done with this white fish. By using white wine, white pepper, and parsley, and then infusing it with the uniquely southwestern taste of New Mexican red chile powder, I've created a dish that is not only tasty but goes with our easy lifestyle.

1 teaspoon olive oil

4 white fish fillets, such as flounder or perch (¾–1 lb. total)

½ cup dry white wine

¼ teaspoon ground white pepper

½ teaspoon New Mexico red chile powder

1 tablespoon minced fresh parsley

GARNISH: *Sprigs of parsley, slices of lemon*

Preheat oven to 400 degrees.

Lightly spread the oil on the bottom of a shallow baking dish and lay the fillets on it. Mix together the wine, pepper, chile powder, and parsley, pour over the fish, and bake in a 400-degree oven for 12 to 15 minutes or until the fish flakes easily when tested with a fork.

Carefully lift the fish out of the poaching liquid, place on a platter or serving plates, garnish with parsley and lemon, and serve.

Serves 4

SERVING SUGGESTIONS: Serve with Summer Salad Greens with Sun-Dried Tomato Vinaigrette (page 86).

CHILE-POACHED COD WITH PEPPER-SHRIMP SAUCE

As early as the late 1800s, smart entrepreneurs were shipping fresh seafood into the Southwest. Although this feat was harder to accomplish before the days of refrigeration, the fresh bounty from the sea was iced down and shipped by rail, with frequent stops for re-icing along the way.

At the turn of the century, restaurants in Albuquerque advertised such delicacies as shrimp, oysters on the half-shell, and all manner of fresh fish, including cod.

Although fish is a great deal easier to get today, we southwesterners still love our imported seafood—especially when we incorporate native ingredients like the apricots, bell peppers, poblanos, and jalapeños that accompany the cod in this dish to make an eye-appealing treat even if the nearest ocean is 500 miles away.

FOR THE PEPPER-SHRIMP SAUCE:

2 tablespoons olive oil

1 large red bell pepper, seeds and membranes removed, sliced into rounds

1 large green bell pepper, seeds and membranes removed, sliced into rounds

1 poblano chile, roasted, peeled, seeded, and chopped

1 red jalapeño, finely chopped (seeded optional)

1 clove garlic, chopped

2 tablespoons fresh lime juice

2 tablespoons white wine

1/2 cup water

1/2 pound small shrimp, peeled and deveined

8–10 large fresh apricots, peeled and seeded

FOR THE CHILE-POACHED COD:

1 cup dry white wine

2 cups water

2 bay leaves

3–4 black peppercorns

1 lime, sliced and seeded

1 tablespoon coarsely chopped fresh parsley

1–1 1/2 pounds codfish steak, 1 inch thick, with the center bone removed

GARNISH: *Lime slices*

To prepare the sauce: Heat the oil in a large saucepan and stir in the bell peppers, poblano, jalapeño, and garlic and sauté for 3 to 4 minutes or until the peppers begin to soften.

Stir in the lime juice, 2 tablespoons of wine, and ½ cup water and bring to a boil. Stir in the shrimp and apricots, reduce the heat, and simmer for 4 to 5 minutes or until the shrimp are cooked. Reduce the heat as low as possible and hold until the cod has finished cooking.

To prepare the cod: While the shrimp are cooking, place 1 cup wine, 2 cups water, the bay leaves, peppercorns, lime, and parsley in a large, deep pan and bring to a boil.

Reduce the heat, add the fish, cover, and cook for 4 to 5 minutes or until the cod flakes easily when tested with a fork. Carefully remove from the poaching liquid, place on serving plates, and sauce with the pepper-shrimp sauce. Garnish with thin slices of lime on the side.

Serves 4

SERVING SUGGESTIONS: Superb served with short-grained rice and thinly sliced pickled ginger.

SHRIMP RIO RANCHO

This vibrant meld of fresh vegetables, amplified by the invigorating bite of green chile, is the perfect showcase for jumbo shrimp.

2 tablespoons olive oil (divided use)

3 medium-size green onions, chopped with the green portion

4 medium-size ripe, red tomatoes, peeled and chopped

2 tablespoons finely chopped fresh parsley

1/2 teaspoon chopped fresh cilantro

1/2 teaspoon salt

1/2 teaspoon ground white pepper

2 New Mexico or Anaheim green chiles, roasted, peeled, seeded, and chopped

1 poblano chile, roasted, peeled, seeded, and chopped

1/2 cup dry (French) vermouth

1 clove garlic, squeezed through a garlic press

24 raw jumbo shrimp, peeled and deveined

GARNISH: *Sprigs of cilantro*

Heat 1 tablespoon of the olive oil in a saucepan and sauté the green onions for 2 to 3 minutes. Add the tomatoes, parsley, cilantro, salt, pepper, chiles, and vermouth and simmer over low heat for about 5 minutes. While it is cooking, pour the remaining 1 tablespoon of oil in a large frying pan with the garlic and let heat. Add the shrimp and cook for 5 to 7 minutes over medium-high heat or until the shrimp turn pink. Spoon the shrimp onto a warmed platter, pour the sauce over them, and garnish with sprigs of cilantro.

Serves 4

SERVING SUGGESTIONS: Serve over hot, cooked brown rice with slices of mango.

SHRIMP SAUTÉED WITH JALAPEÑO AND TEQUILA

Shrimp is so versatile and easy to prepare, yet always makes an elegant meal. No matter where you are when you taste this spirited combination of shrimp, jalapeño, and tequila with the crunch of sesame seeds, close your eyes and you will think you are basking on a lovely Mexican beach.

2 tablespoons olive oil

3 green onions, finely chopped with some of the green portion

2 cloves garlic, squeezed through a garlic press

1 tablespoon finely chopped fresh parsley

1 pound jumbo shrimp (16–20 count), peeled and deveined

¼ cup all-purpose flour

¼ cup dry white wine

1 tablespoon fresh lemon juice

1 tablespoon gold (aged) tequila

¼ teaspoon ground white pepper

1 jalapeño, finely chopped

¼ cup toasted sesame seeds

GARNISH: *Sprigs of cilantro or parsley*

Heat the oil in a frying pan and sauté the green onions, garlic, and parsley for 2 to 3 minutes. Lightly flour the shrimp and cook over medium heat for 5 to 7 minutes or until they are just done. Remove the shrimp and reserve in a warm oven. Add the wine, lemon juice, tequila, pepper, and jalapeño to the frying pan and simmer for 3 to 4 minutes. Remove the shrimp from the oven, pour the sauce over the shrimp, sprinkle the sesame seeds over the top, garnish with cilantro or parsley, and serve.

Serves 4

SERVING SUGGESTIONS: Serve with saffron rice and French bread, lightly spread with basil pesto and broiled until lightly toasted.

SHRIMP MARINATED IN A CHILE "MARTINI"

Marinating the shrimp in this "martini" (in which the proportions of vermouth and gin are reversed and then spiked with pequín chile) before grilling gives the shrimp a delightful flavor. You need only a little crushed chile, as I've found through my decidedly unscientific research that the gin seems to intensify the heat of the chile.

½ cup fresh lemon juice

½ cup dry (French) vermouth

2 tablespoons gin

1 tablespoon Worcestershire sauce

½ teaspoon crushed pequín chile

1 clove garlic, chopped

3 green onions, green portion only, finely chopped

1 tablespoon chopped fresh parsley

24 jumbo shrimp (approx. 1¼ lb. total), peeled and deveined

Simmer the lemon juice, vermouth, gin, Worcestershire sauce, pequín chile, and garlic for 5 or 6 minutes over low heat, stirring constantly. Stir in the onion and parsley.

Place the shrimp in a shallow glass bowl. Pour the "martini"-chile mixture over the shrimp and marinate for 5 minutes. (Any longer and the shrimp will "cook" too long in the marinade.)

Broil the shrimp on a stovetop grill or over charcoal for 3 to 4 minutes or until done, brushing the marinade over them at least twice during the cooking.

Serves 4

SERVING SUGGESTIONS: Serve on a bed of greens or mixed lettuce with sliced fresh fruit arranged around the edge of the plate.

GRILLED SHRIMP MARINATED IN LIME AND RED CHILE WITH MELON SALSA

The smell of the lime juice and the crushed chile in this dish might make you want to leave the shrimp in the marinade more than 15 minutes. Resist the temptation, as the shrimp will "cook" in the marinade if left too long.

The fresh, summery taste of the melon salsa provides an enticing counterpoint to the briny, hot taste of the grilled shrimp.

FOR THE SHRIMP AND MARINADE:

1 pound large shrimp (16–20 count), peeled and deveined

¼ cup fresh lime juice

½ cup white wine

1 clove garlic, minced

1–2 teaspoons crushed árbol chiles

1 tablespoon chopped fresh cilantro

½ teaspoon freshly ground black pepper

FOR THE SALSA:

1 cup diced, peeled, and seeded cantaloupe

1 cup diced, peeled, and seeded honeydew melon

1 cup diced, peeled, and seeded Persian or crenshaw melon

1 Anaheim or New Mexico green chile, roasted, peeled, and chopped

2 tablespoons fresh lime juice

1 tablespoon fresh chopped cilantro

To prepare the shrimp: Place the shrimp in a glass bowl, stir in the marinade ingredients, cover, and marinate at room temperature for 15 minutes. Remove from the marinade and grill the shrimp for 3 to 4 minutes or until done, basting at least once with the marinade. Discard the marinade.

To prepare the salsa: Mix all the salsa ingredients together and refrigerate for 1 hour before serving. This salsa will not keep well for more than a day.

Serves 4

SERVING SUGGESTIONS: Accompany with risotto, grilled corn, or grilled potato slices.

ANGEL HAIR PASTA WITH SHRIMP, POBLANO, AND SERRANO CHILE

When people ask me what my favorite dish is, I never hesitate to tell them about this recipe. The delicate angel hair pasta makes a perfect host to the fresh-from-the-sea taste of the shrimp and the searing heat of the serrano and poblano chiles.

I often use a pasta made with a combination of Jerusalem artichokes and wheat. It is available in gourmet sections of supermarkets and in health food stores. I find that it has a more delicate flavor and texture than the angel-hair made with hard wheat flour.

12 ounces angel hair pasta (preferably made with Jerusalem artichokes)

3 tablespoons olive oil

2 cloves garlic, minced

1 tablespoon chopped fresh parsley

1 large-size pimento or red bell pepper, seeds and membranes removed, chopped

1 poblano chile, roasted, peeled, seeded, and chopped

1 serrano chile, seeded and chopped

¼ cup sliced black olives

½ teaspoon freshly ground black pepper

½ pound small to medium shrimp, peeled, deveined, and cooked

GARNISH: *Chopped fresh basil leaves, freshly grated Romano or Parmesan cheese (optional)*

Cook the pasta according to package directions. While it is cooking, heat the olive oil, stir in the garlic, parsley, and pimento, and sauté for 3 to 4 minutes. Stir in the poblano and serrano chiles, olives, black pepper, and shrimp, and cook until the shrimp are warm. Drain the pasta, spoon the shrimp sauce over it, toss, and serve with chopped fresh basil or freshly grated Romano or Parmesan cheese, if desired.

Serves 4

SERVING SUGGESTIONS: This pasta makes a wonderful first course or a great main dish served with sliced, toasted bolillos.

LINGUINE WITH SCALLOPS AND ANAHEIM CHILE

The burnt adobe color of the tomato-basil pasta in this dish provides a sharp contrast to the savory and colorful sauce of green chile, black olives, and red pimento that houses the scallops.

12 ounces tomato-basil linguine

3 tablespoons olive oil

2 cloves garlic, minced

1 tablespoon chopped fresh parsley

1 pimento, roasted, peeled, seeded, and chopped

2 medium-size Anaheim or New Mexico green chiles, roasted, peeled, seeded, and chopped

¼ cup sliced black olives

½ teaspoon freshly ground black pepper

1 pound small scallops (if you can find only large ones, quarter them before using)

GARNISH: *Chopped fresh basil*

Cook the linguine according to package directions. While it is cooking, heat the oil in a large frying pan, stir in the garlic, parsley, and pimento and sauté for 3 to 4 minutes. Stir in the chiles, olives, pepper, and scallops and cook for 5 to 6 minutes or until the scallops turn opaque and are just done. Drain the linguine, spoon the scallops and chile sauce over it, toss, and garnish with chopped fresh basil.

Serves 4

SERVING SUGGESTIONS: Start the meal with a cup of corn chowder, followed by the pasta and topped off with peaches poached in white wine and raspberry liqueur.

SPAGHETTINI WITH CLAMS AND ÁRBOL CHILE

The clams, red chile, and cilantro give a new meaning to eating "spaghetti." This is a nice, lighter change from the classic linguine and clam sauce and yet has an excellent depth of flavor due to the addition of those southwestern favorites, cilantro and chile.

3 cloves garlic, quartered

½ teaspoon crushed árbol chile

26 small clams, well scrubbed

2 cups dry white wine

1 cup water

1 tablespoon chopped fresh cilantro

1 tablespoon chopped fresh parsley

2 tablespoons chopped fresh basil

½ teaspoon salt

½ teaspoon freshly ground black pepper

1 pound spaghettini

GARNISH: *Sprigs of cilantro or parsley*

Place the garlic, chile, clams, wine, and water in a large saucepan, cover, and bring to a boil. Reduce the heat and cook the clams for 6 to 8 minutes or until the clams open. Discard any clams that do not open.

Using a slotted spoon, remove the clams and set aside. Bring the pan juices back to a boil and cook for 4 to 5 minutes until reduced slightly. Reduce the heat, stir in the cilantro, parsley, basil, salt, and pepper and simmer.

Cook the spaghettini in boiling water for 7 to 8 minutes or until done. While the pasta is cooking, remove the clams from their shells and add to the saucepan.

When the pasta is cooked, drain and place on a large serving plate or spaghetti platter. Pour the sauce over the pasta, and garnish with sprigs of cilantro or parsley.

Serves 4–6

SERVING SUGGESTIONS: Serve with French bread that has been spread with a sun-dried tomato and basil pesto and lightly browned under the broiler.

CRAB, PAPAYA, AND AVOCADO ENCHILADAS

After a hard, albeit exhilarating, day demonstrating cooking to novices or explaining the merits of my latest book to the patrons of a crowded bookstore, I can think of nothing more comforting than an enchilada for supper.

I developed my first crab enchilada in the early 1970s; now they are the "in" thing. The addition of the papaya teamed with the poblano chile gives this dish a sweet, piquant flavor.

2 tablespoons olive oil

1 small-size white onion, diced

2 cloves garlic, finely chopped

1½ pounds cooked crabmeat, picked over and washed, shredded

1 tablespoon chopped fresh cilantro

1 ripe papaya, peeled, seeded, and diced

3 poblano chiles, roasted, peeled, seeded, and diced

¼ teaspoon salt

½ teaspoon freshly ground black pepper

12 corn tortillas (5 inches in diameter)

2 cups Red Chile Sauce (recipe, page 114)

2 avocados, peeled, seeded, and sliced

½ cup shredded Monterey Jack cheese

GARNISH: *Fat-free sour cream, sliced black olives, sprigs of cilantro*

Heat the olive oil in a saucepan and sauté the onion, garlic, crabmeat, cilantro, papaya, chile, salt, and pepper until the onions are translucent.

Preheat oven to 350 degrees.

Dip the corn tortillas, one at a time, in the Red Chile Sauce.

Divide the crab and chile mixture fold into 12 servings and spoon 1 serving down the center of each tortilla. Add avocado slices. Fold the tortilla and place in a glass baking dish that has been rubbed with oil. Pour the remaining sauce in the dish and sprinkle the cheese on top. Cover with aluminum foil and bake in a 350-degree oven for 20 minutes or until the cheese has melted and the enchilada is heated through. Place 2 or 3 enchiladas on each serving plate, spoon a dollop of fat-free sour cream on top, sprinkle sliced black olives on top of that, and garnish with a sprig of cilantro.

Serves 4–6

SERVING SUGGESTIONS: Serve with cooked pinto beans and confetti rice.

INDEX